Already Ready
Nurturing Writers in Preschool and Kindergarten

Katie Wood Ray *and* Matt Glover

HEINEMANN © PORTSMOUTH, NH

Heinemann

A division of Reed Elsevier Inc.

361 Hanover Street

Portsmouth, NH 03801–3912

www.heinemann.com

Offices and agents throughout the world

Library of Congress Cataloging-in-Publication Data

Ray, Katie Wood.

   Already ready : nurturing writers in preschool and kindergarten / Katie Wood Ray and Matt Glover.

      p. cm.

   Includes bibliographical references and index.

   ISBN-13: 978-0-325-01073-1

   ISBN-10: 0-325-01073-0

   1. Language arts (Early childhood).   2. Creative writing.   I. Glover, Matt.
II. Title.

   LB1139.5.L35R395   2008

   372.62′3—dc22
                                       2007035319

Editor: Kate Montgomery

Production: Elizabeth Valway

Interior and cover designs: Jenny Jensen Greenleaf

Cover photo by Alex Mares-Manton

Part 1 opener photo by Patty Geroni

Part 2 opener photo by Penny Cecil

Composition: House of Equations, Inc.

Manufacturing: Steve Bernier

Printed in the United States of America on acid-free paper

12 11 10 09 08 VP 1 2 3 4 5

For Jim Ray, again, and still.

—K.W.R.

*For Bridget, and for my favorite authors—
Harrison, Meredith, Molly, and Natalie.*

—M.G.

Contents

Foreword

■■■■■■■■■■■■■■■■■■■■■■■■■■■■■■■■■■■■■■

From the very first chapter of this informative and inspiring book, a clear picture emerges of how even three- and four-year-olds' capacities for serious authorship can and should be supported. Easily visualized examples of the daily events in the classroom and the children's responses to their many opportunities to "make books" are offered throughout. Katie Ray and Matt Glover share with us their rich, extensive, firsthand experience of helping preschoolers to become increasingly competent authors of books of various genres.

Ray and Glover present their powerful ideas and suggestions in two parts. The first helps us understand at a very profound level what it means to be a writer, the nature of authorship development during the early years, and the complexities of what is required to support it. A wide range of illustrations of children's first authorship efforts is included throughout the book.

The second part offers an exceptionally detailed set of general strategies and specific techniques teachers can use to initiate young children's authorship. Included here are not only ample suggestions concerning how to organize the classroom, but also many useful and practical examples of teacher responses to children as they progress through the different authorship stages.

The authors' insights, based on extensive direct experiences, are first-rate examples of the important distinction between *knowing about* a child and *knowing* a child—for it is clear that the responsive actions and thoughtfully determined inactions of the teachers depend on really knowing the individual child involved in a particular teachable moment. As they point out, supporting children in the act of composition involves truly complex combinations of processes, each of which is effectively described and illustrated using real interactions with preschoolers in their classrooms. Cautions about the common temptation to overassist the very young, which is familiar to all of us, are explored and explained. The interesting distinction the authors make between "nudging" and pushing children is one of many such suggestions in their reports about actual experiences in the classroom. In addition, the words of the children themselves and many of their individual products included are convincing and helpful in providing insight into how to teach authorship to preschoolers.

The rich illustrations of preschoolers becoming authors offered here could not have come at a better time—a time when so many in decision-making and policy-making roles underestimate children's intellectual capacities. They are the ones who require us to focus instead on doing earlier and earlier to children what we probably shouldn't do to them later; that is, even teachers of young children are increasingly under great pressure to prepare them to master academic skills so that they can perform well on standardized tests.

I suggest that it is useful for all educators to keep the distinction between *academic* and *intellectual* aspects of development and learning in mind. Academic goals are served by presenting children with worksheets, drills, and other kinds of exercises designed to get them started on basic literacy and numeracy skills. Academic tasks consist mainly of small, dissembedded items, usually taught in isolation, require right answers, rely heavily on rote learning versus understanding, and are mastered from formal instruction in which learners are in a passive role. Such instruction is more focused on the regurgitation of specific items than on deepening understanding. Such skills clearly have an important place in education as children get older but perhaps not for preschoolers.

Intellectual goals and activities, on the other hand, are focused on the life of the mind in its fullest sense, including its aesthetic and moral sensibilities. The formal definition of the term *intellectual* emphasizes reasoning, processes of reflection, development and analyses of observations and ideas, and other creative active uses of the mind. They also include the dispositions to theorize and to hypothesize about cause–effect relationships; to make predictions and to check them; to wonder, to question, to investigate, and to pry; and to find out things. It is both reasonable and useful for teachers to assume that these intellectual dispositions are common in all children—granted stronger in some than in others. Furthermore, it is possible that excessive and premature emphasis on academic skills may damage the in-born intellectual dispositions that can flourish by applying the teaching strategies and practical principles clearly presented and exemplified here.

Along similar lines, another reason why this book is so welcome and timely is that it makes a very convincing case for the benefits of providing young children with opportunities to be active and interactive rather than passive and reactive in the learning environment. In addition, their active roles support a wide variety of learning—learning about authors and genres, how to "read" their books to others, and very much more. The authors' insistence on talking to children about "book-making" rather than just writing is based on their conviction that the process of making something involves setting out to accomplish something—something intentional. Further, with rich examples, they point out that authorship often leads to many new understandings about many aspects of literacy. The vividness of the descriptions of the teacher's role will be readily grasped by those not yet teaching but still in the process of training.

Each chapter includes a summary of the main points that clearly indicates the practical implications and applications described and discussed in it. The summaries certainly will help those who work with preschoolers get started on what could become a lifelong disposition to express their ideas and understandings with intention and clarity and satisfaction.

—Lilian G. Katz, Ph.D.
Professor Emerita of Early Childhood Education and
Co-Director, ERIC Clearinghouse on Elementary & Early Childhood
Education Children's Research Center

Acknowledgments

▪▪▪▪▪▪▪▪▪▪▪▪▪▪▪▪▪▪▪▪▪▪▪▪▪▪▪▪▪▪▪▪▪▪▪▪▪▪▪

We would like to thank all the Lakota Local School District preschool teachers and therapists who have been so willing to invite us into their classrooms the past several years: classroom teachers Susan Bolander, Cindy Brausch-Knemeyer, Sharon Byrnes, Penny Cecil, Heather Chaney, Marlene Cooley, Cheryl Fuertges, Patty Geroni, Pam Heidorn, Kate McHugh, Natalie Messmer, Joanne Muir-Myers, Pat Schmees, Cindy Trimbell, Keri Turner, and Jennie Webbink; preschool speech pathologists Melissa Adolph, Jana Borgemenke, Angie Bryant, Susan Farnell, Sara Fielder, April Grahl, Diane Keene, Mara Ottke, Cara Pease, Joyce Smith, Peg Wernersbach, and Emily Yount. This book could not have been written if it weren't for your generous collaborations.

A special thank-you goes to all the preschool writers who wowed us again and again. You taught us so much.

Pat Mascaritolo and Peggy Banet—thank you for your willingness to talk passionately with Matt about young children and their thinking.

Thank you to literacy specialists Mary Alice Berry, Mari Pumphrey, Laura Sites, Asha Ruiz, and Emily Speed for your dedication to supporting young children's literacy and for always thinking about the best ways to nurture learning.

Bobbie Bach, Tara Eddy, Kathy Keyes, and Chris Caster—thank you all, not just for always making everything work, but also for understanding what's important for young children.

Thank you to past and current Lakota Local School District leaders Kathy Klink, Mike Taylor, Cecilia Schmidt, and Vicki Curtis for creating an environment that invites and encourages growth and innovation

We would like to thank Katie's study group—Mark Hardy, Gaby Layden, and Isoke Titilayo Nia—for reading early chapters and responding so thoughtfully. Amy Ludwig-Vanderwater also read early drafts. Thank you, Amy. Your feedback was invaluable.

Rita Hoppert and Gretchen Estreicher—thank you for supporting opportunities to share this work with others. And a special thanks to the Cincinnati Public preschool teachers and other seminar participants for your conversations and reactions to ideas.

Thank you Ena Shelley and Kathy Roskos for your meaningful conversations with Matt about young children and for so graciously sharing your thinking.

Thanks to all the people at Heinemann who support the development of professional resources such as this one, and especially to our editor, Kate Montgomery.

Matt thanks Bridget Glover, one of the best natural teachers he knows. Bridget's conversations and solid, grounded thinking have so enriched this book; and her patience and understanding allowed Matt to coauthor successfully in his "spare" time. And thank you to Matt's children—Harrison, Meredith, Molly, and Natalie—for helping us see so many possibilities.

Katie would like to thank Jim Ray for his continued support of her work, for ten years of partnership, and for planting all the wonderful things outside her new office. Every time she looks out her window, she's reminded just how lucky she is.

Introduction

■■■■■■■■■■■■■■■■■■■■■■■■■■■■■■■■■

It's the thinking that gets us every time.

On a single day in May, privileged as we were to be sitting alongside preschool writers who were making picture books, we saw children engaged in the most amazing thinking. In squiggled lines moving from front to back, Kee illustrated the sound of a siren coming from a fire truck (Figure I.1). Evan made the eyes of his dinosaur slant sideways to show it looking back while running away from an erupting volcano (Figure I.2). On the cover of a book about going to a Build-a-Bear Workshop®, Lilly drew only the backs of people's heads to show they are entering the store (Figure I.3). And Nolan added lines to the page in his book illustrating a home run. The lines traced the path of the ball from the pitcher to the bat to the outfield, and then captured the player's speedy spin around the bases (Figure I.4).

It's the thinking we can't get away from, and a mutual fascination with the intellectual lives of preschoolers is what brought us together around this work.

We, Katie Ray and Matt Glover, met several years ago in a professional development setting. At the time, Katie was a teacher-educator, writer, and researcher (she still is); and Matt was the principal of a large early childhood school (he still is too). As the instructional leader at his school, Matt had become very involved in a study of children's writing development with the kindergarten teachers. Katie had coauthored one of the professional resources used in that study—*About the Authors: Writing Workshop with Our Youngest Writers* (2004). Following a framing idea from the book, Matt and the teachers began inviting children to make picture books with writing, and they studied what happened when kindergarteners composed in this context. What they saw was not surprising: Children engaged in complex, sophisticated thinking as they used writing to make books. At the time, Matt told Katie he couldn't agree more with a statement from the introduction to *About the Authors*:

FIG. I.1 *Kee's Fire Truck*

FIG. I.2 *Evan's Dinosaur*

FIG. I.3 *Lilly's Build-a-Bear Workshop®*

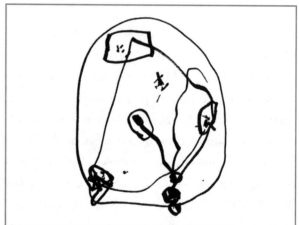

FIG. I.4 *Nolan's Homerun Page*

Our work has grown, instead, from a *fascination* with children's development as writers. We have seen again and again that when we get those markers and that paper in their hands, worlds of possibilities simply open up for all kinds of interesting development that feels natural and joyful and absolutely appropriate. We believe that curriculum that follows these possibilities is a "shoved-up" curriculum, pushed upon us as teachers when young children show us what they are capable of doing. (x)

The project-like nature of children's book-making was a natural fit in Matt's school. For years, teachers there had studied the intellectual growth of children and learned from numerous educators involved in research about young children, including those at Reggio Emilia where, as Howard Gardner (1998) describes: "The principal educational vehicle involves youngsters in long-term engrossing projects, which are carried out in a beautiful, healthy, love-filled setting" (xvi). As writing itself became more project-like, teachers recognized the familiar energy that comes from being so "engrossed."

Seeing the energy so many children brought to writing and book-making in kindergarten, and seeing the amazing thinking children engaged in as they composed in this context, it wasn't long before Matt and some of the other teachers began wondering, "What if we extended the invitation to make books to preschoolers? What might happen if three- and four-year-olds got paper and markers in their hands and were invited to make books with them?" The wondering led some teachers to present book-making as an invitation in their preschool classes. To support the professional development of these teachers, Matt began coteaching in the preschool classrooms, helping the teachers study what happened when children responded to the invitation to make books.

Two or three times a week when Matt arrived home from school, he emailed Katie to tell her about his experiences with preschoolers who were making books. Her interest was piqued, to say the least, so Matt began videotaping his interactions with children and sent the videos to Katie. He felt like having "another set of eyes" studying these interactions could help him and the teachers he was supporting "see" more of what was happening in the classrooms. As we played and replayed the videotaped data, we shared our insights and anomalies.

Working together, our thinking grew, as did our profound respect for the capacity of children to thoughtfully compose. We found ourselves exactly where Loris Malaguzzi, founding father of the Reggio Emilia schools, said we would find ourselves:

> All people—and I mean scholars, researchers, and teachers, who in any place have set themselves to study children seriously—have ended up by discovering not so much the limits and weaknesses of children but rather their surprising and extraordinary strengths and capabilities linked with an inexhaustible need for expression and realization. (1998, 78)

At some point we both knew and said, "We have to write about this." So, we set out on the journey that has led us to this book. For two years, Matt supported the preschool teachers in his school by teaching alongside them several days a week in a large number of classrooms. The children he encountered represented a wide spectrum of development because every preschool classroom there is evenly divided between children who are identified as typically developing and those who have special needs. As he spent time in classrooms, Matt collected a variety of data: written artifacts (mostly children's writing), field notes, and more than fifty hours of videotaped interactions with children. He used this data to support professional conversations with the school's teachers, and together we used it to deepen our understandings about young writers, to refine our teaching practices, and eventually to describe this work in ways we hope other teachers will find helpful.

With a very narrow focus on writing development, *Already Ready: Nurturing Writers in Preschool and Kindergarten* is a book written for teaching professionals who work with young children. The first five chapters make up the "Building Understandings About Young Writers" part and explain what we believe are some fundamental understandings about the writing development of young children. From these understandings, teaching practice evolves and the second part, also five chapters, focuses on this practice. Part Two, "Teaching Practices That Nurture Young Writers," explores three familiar contexts—read-aloud, side-by-side teaching, and share time—for nurturing young writers. In between each of the ten chapters, we've included short "Meet the Author and Illustrator" segments where we introduce you to some three- and four-year-old authors and the stories behind some of their writing.

We realize that if this book were all a person knew about preschools, that person might think that they are places where children go to learn how to write. After all, the focus of this book is on writing, and we've tried to stay, well, focused on that. But in truth, writing and the development of writers is not *the* focus of preschool classrooms; it's only one important focal point among many, and a fairly narrow one at that, even in terms of literacy development. Such a narrow focus won't teach someone all she or he needs to know to work with young children. Instead, a narrow focus affords teachers the opportunity to dig deeply enough into something so that they come out understanding it in a very grounded way. We hope that the narrow focus of this book will help teachers do just that.

Children's Writing

Already Ready is filled with examples of three- and four-year-olds' writing. Our hope is that by including so many examples, we have adequately represented a range of writing development that is typical of preschool children. The writings are important for another reason too. If we had written only about the thinking children engage in as they compose without including the writing artifacts, some might have a difficult time believing we are actually discussing the writing of children this young. Without a doubt, the written products alone belie the richly layered, complex thinking that stands behind them. They may not look like much, but so much is there that you cannot see. Therefore, to understand either the thinking or the writing with any depth, it's essential to examine both closely.

Because the children are not here to represent the meanings in their writing to you on their own terms, and because most of their writing is not yet representational on its own, you will find written transcripts for most of their writings. Presented with quotation marks around them, these transcripts capture the oral readings children composed for their books. However, we should stress that making transcripts of children's oral readings is not a *classroom* practice we embrace. Our reasoning for this is explained in detail later in the book. Instead of adults transcribing children's words for them, in the classrooms where children make books, the young writers and illustrators are allowed to represent meanings on their own terms, and they're celebrated for doing their best with the writing and illustrating knowledge they have at this point in their development. Children read and reread their books, and their readings come only from what *they* have represented on paper. No adult writing is there. But when they are not present, transcripts give adults access to children's composing and the thinking behind it and serve an important function in this book for that purpose.

As you look at and enjoy the children's writing throughout the book, we invite you to think of the transcripts as soundtracks and imagine the children reading their books to you in their best read-aloud voices.

A Note About the Book's Title

Finally, we'd like to explain a little of the thinking that led to the title of this book, *Already Ready: Nurturing Writers in Preschool and Kindergarten*. The hope for titles, like names for anything we suppose—children, pets, boats—is that they will capture some of the spirit of what they name. We certainly hope this is true of this book's title, and a few words hold particular significance.

First, *Already Ready*. The notion of readiness is an idea that is just beneath the surface of every discussion about young writers throughout the book, so its place in the title seemed essential to us. We operate from a core belief that children do not need to "get ready" to be readers and writers; instead, we believe they are already readers and writers—albeit on their own terms—as they live and learn inside literate communities.

Second, the word *nurture* holds critical meaning in the title. In our computer dictionary, we find these definitions for the verb *nurture*:

1. to give tender care and protection to a child, a young animal, or a plant, helping it to grow and develop;

2. to encourage somebody or something to grow, develop, thrive, and be successful;

3. to keep a feeling in the mind for a long time, allowing it to grow or deepen.

The word simply captures both the meaning and the spirit of the adult's role in this work with young children. After all, this book is not about *teaching writing*, it's about *nurturing writers*. This difference is critical. The verbs suggest different actions, and the objects of the verbs suggest very different purposes behind those actions.

Although this book was written as a result of experiences with writers who were in preschools, in truth, much of what we've learned has nothing to do with children this age. In particular, becoming articulate about composition development has refined our understandings of working with children at any developmental level. Realizing the need to *nurture* children's growing understandings about texts, process, and what it means to be a writer has helped us realize new possibilities for the kinds of work we might do with students across all grade levels.

In addition, and perhaps most important, this work with the youngest writers has taught us to see so much more in the thinking children are doing behind their writing. We know that training our eyes to see more in children's writing will impact our teaching of all students regardless of their experience as writers. Truly, then, we believe this book is about nurturing writers in preschool, kindergarten, and *beyond*, and we hope readers of it will agree.

PART ONE

Building Understandings About Young Writers

Meet Kyle

Author and Illustrator of Fire Engine

As a three-year-old, Kyle was already reading at a fairly high level and could talk at length on a variety of subjects of interest to him, from music to cooking to making books—he was quite the Renaissance man already. Like many three-year-olds, Kyle loved being silly, giggling, and playing with his friends. Not surprisingly, his fine-motor skills were more typical of a three-year-old and not quite as developed as his language skills.

Kyle loved making books, even though he knew he couldn't yet represent all he wanted in his illustrations. Fortunately, he was very comfortable with his own approximations, and fortunately for his teachers, his approximations helped them see the many things he knew about books, authors, and illustrators.

Kyle certainly understood what it means to read like a writer. One day his teacher read Donald Crews' wonderful book *Freight Train* with the specific intention of looking at the decisions Crews made as the illustrator. The teacher and children looked at how the first several pages showed a track without a train and wondered together why Donald hadn't included the train on these pages. They discussed how the illustrator made the train look like it was going slow on one page and fast on another. They thought about how Crews showed that it was night toward the end. And while the teacher would occasionally mention that children could try these things in their books, she was primarily interested in supporting their habit of noticing.

Kyle was obviously listening carefully. He went over to the writing table and began making a book about a fire engine. As he was working on the first page, his teacher asked him about the different parts of a fire truck and where they were in his illustration. Kyle added sirens, ladders, lights, and even the button you push to make the *beep-beep* sound the truck makes when it's backing up. He also took a risk and added a title, *Fire Engine*, with marks at the top of the page that were different from the swirling marks he typically used for writing.

On the next page Kyle asked his teacher, "Do you see any fire trucks on this page?" He eagerly awaited her expected reply.

"Well, no. Is there a truck?" she asked.

"No, the truck isn't there yet," Kyle responded, and then he went back to working on his book, confident his teacher would understand he was trying to be like Donald Crews. The book is rich with details and deep thinking that the illustrations don't convey on their own.

Teachers are well aware of the amazing growth children make over a year, but it is especially apparent with Kyle. A page from a book Kyle made a year later about a trip to Florida follows. Kyle's motor skills are catching up to his writing and oral language skills. What a shame it would have been to wait until this point to begin nurturing his development as a writer.

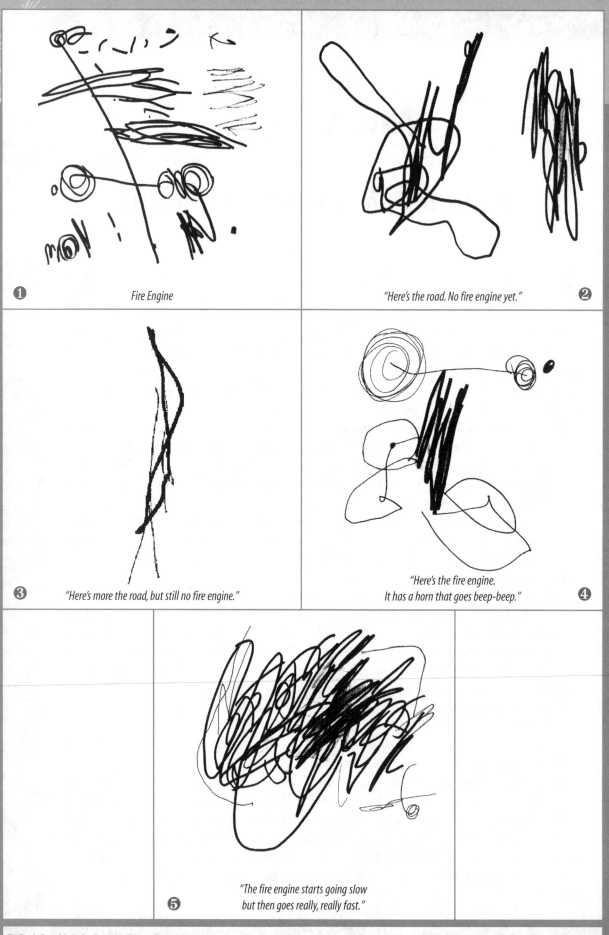

① *Fire Engine*

② *"Here's the road. No fire engine yet."*

③ *"Here's more the road, but still no fire engine."*

④ *"Here's the fire engine. It has a horn that goes beep-beep."*

⑤ *"The fire engine starts going slow but then goes really, really fast."*

FIG. 1.2 **Kyle's Book, Fire Engine**

"We were running fast to catch the plane."

FIG. 1.3   *A Page from Kyle's Book About a Trip to Florida*

Composition and the Importance of Making Picture Books

■■■

In a preschool classroom, Matt and Shruthi are having a conversation about twelve dancing princesses, the topic of Shruthi's latest book. All around them in the classroom, children are involved in different kinds of activities, and in the background is the predictable hum of three- and four-year-olds busy doing things. At one point, Matt and Shruthi are interrupted as a child brings Matt a hot dog that she says she's made him for lunch. On the other side of the table, Jeffrey comes up and begins working quite independently on a book about his dog, Pepper. He works his way through all the pages, and in the end, he reads his book to Matt (Figure 2.1).

In many ways, this scene is typical of preschool classrooms everywhere: Children are actively engaged and adults are interacting with them around those engagements. Indeed, all the work with children we describe in this book takes place in fairly typical preschool classrooms in this sense. The children attend half-day sessions, and for the two-and-a-half hours they're there, they choose from a variety of hands-on experiences that support their growth across a wide spectrum of development. This chapter considers how a scene like this comes to be. What is in place in this classroom that sets in motion the experience Jeffrey had as a writer on this morning? And why this particular experience—the making of a picture book?

Focused Experiences

What makes preschool classrooms distinct, of course, are the decisions adults are making about what experiences children should be having. The focus at the

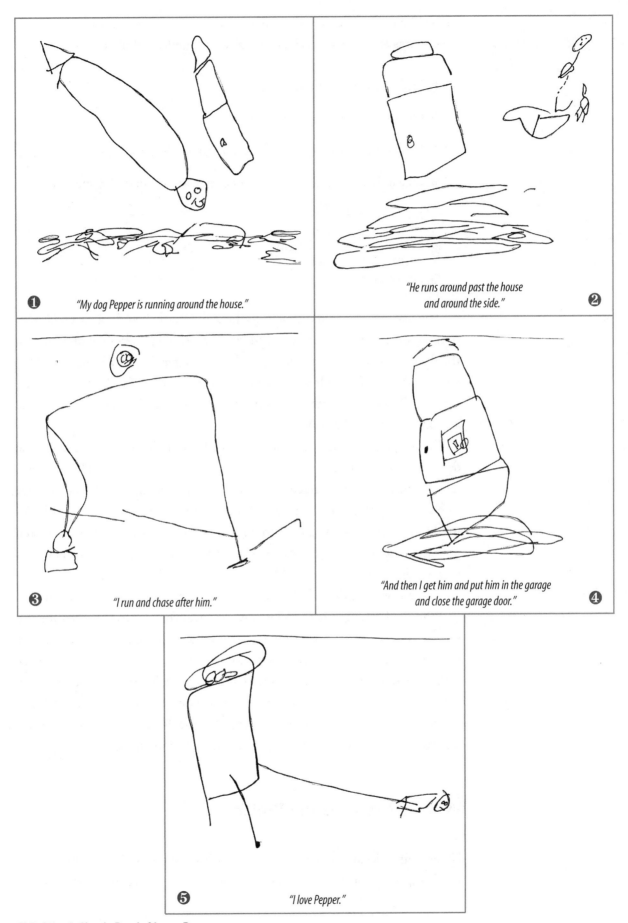

1. "My dog Pepper is running around the house."

2. "He runs around past the house and around the side."

3. "I run and chase after him."

4. "And then I get him and put him in the garage and close the garage door."

5. "I love Pepper."

FIG. 2.1 *Jeffrey's Book About Pepper*

early childhood center Jeffrey attends is on creating classrooms where children's experiences lead to the development of seven intellectual dispositions:

- Problem solving and reasoning

- Questioning and problem posing

- Keen observation—gathering data through all the senses

- Imagining, innovating, and responding with wonderment and awe

- Intellectual risk-taking

- Thinking interdependently

- Persistence

The teachers and administrators at the center settled on these seven dispositions as a guiding focus for their work after reviewing professional literature on the development of habits of mind in young children (Costa and Kallick 2000; Helm and Katz 2001; Edwards, Gandini, and Forman 1998). As defined in the center's mission statement, "dispositions go beyond the skill and emphasize the attitude to use a skill productively."

The emphasis on attitudes and using skills in productive ways leads to the development of many projects, both large and small, at the center. This past year, for example, one of the preschool classes worked for many months on a project to buy and install a small ornamental pond at the school so that their tadpoles would have a safe place to grow into frogs. The children were involved every step of the way, from researching pond possibilities, to securing donations and volunteers, to unpacking and eventually installing the pond on school grounds.

Reading, writing, drawing, listening, and speaking—all are essential to projects like this, and through them children experience what it's like to need literacy skills to accomplish goals. On any given day at the early childhood center, it's not uncommon to see children and teachers doing things such as reading directions, making lists, writing notes, sketching observations, explaining to each other how something is done, or asking for help or information from outside sources. In projects large and small, children are encouraged to use the skills of literacy—including writing, of course—in meaningful ways to support their projects.

When Writing *Is* the Project

When Jeffrey decides to make a book about his dog, Pepper, he is using writing not to support another project but as a project itself. Considering this, it's help-

writing that requires mostly transcription before nudging children to use writing in a compositional sense? The reason is, quite simply, that transcription is not a prerequisite for compositional writing. It's a *part of* compositional writing, but not a prerequesite.

A writer like Jeffrey can think about all the things he needs to think about to make something with writing—about purpose, ideas, organization, word choices, craft, genre, tone, audience, presentation, and on and on—whether he can transcribe them accurately or not. If a writer doesn't know anything about how to get the words down yet, he just uses other means to capture all the thinking he's doing while composing. Some of it he captures on paper with illustrations, some of it he captures in his memory with repeated readings, and some of it he captures by reading it to other people—creating a shared memory that holds his thinking way better than his memory alone. Writers like Jeffrey are quite capable of doing the thinking work of composition before they know how to transcribe; it's really no problem at all.

As a matter of fact, not knowing much about transcription actually frees writers to put more thinking energy into other aspects of writing. Once children know more about how to get words down, they'll necessarily be distracted by this knowledge and will put more of their thinking energy into transcription for quite some time. They won't be able to help it; this transcription "distraction" is developmentally inevitable for writers. But when teachers expose children right from the start to composition, allowing them to experience what it's like to make something with writing, they're helping them develop the idea of using the skill of writing productively long before the skill itself is mastered.

Inviting children to compose with writing also helps them build much stronger identities as writers. Experiencing the response of readers, in particular, helps children understand the power they hold when they compose and "arrange things to achieve a particular effect." Imagine how Jeffrey's understanding of what he's accomplished with his book is enhanced when he shares it and a teacher responds:

> Oh my. You must have been so scared when Pepper got loose and
> you couldn't catch him. I know how scary that is. My dog Montana
> got loose like that once and I was so afraid he wouldn't come back.
> You must have felt so much better when you finally closed that
> garage door.

People who don't use writing to compose probably don't realize the significance of a response like that as much as people who do. To writers, responses that show they've "achieved a particular effect"—especially if it's the effect they intended—are critical in terms of helping them believe they can use writing to get things done in the world.

The distinction we are making, then, between functional writing and compositional writing is not one of value. Both are equally valued as literate commodities. The distinction we are making is meant to help adults working with young children broaden the scope of what's possible for them as writers. Understanding that composition requires writers to take a different stance to writing, teachers can consider new invitations that encourage children to compose and make things with writing just as experienced writers do.

In Jeffrey's classroom, his teachers privilege and encourage book-making as a literacy experience because it involves children in the thinking process of composition, and they've made time, space, and materials available so that children can choose to make books whenever they like. But why the emphasis on picture books, you may be wondering. The answer to this question is significant in understanding what brought Jeffrey to the table on this morning to make his book, and we'll consider it next.

Why Make Picture Books?

Picture Books Are Familiar

The first reason teachers encourage the making of picture books is because they are a familiar kind of writing to very young children. Even if children don't see them much at home, at school teachers share picture books in read-alouds at least once and sometimes more than once a day. The books are shared in whole-class, small-group, and one-on-one settings. Children are also encouraged to spend time with picture books on their own if they'd like, and usually a wide variety of them can be found in any preschool classroom.

Because they are so familiar, children don't have trouble imagining what it means to make a picture book. Contrast this familiarity with something like a journal—a kind of writing most children have no experience with as readers. Even single pieces of paper for drawing and writing are not a publishing format children will see anywhere else in the world of writing. The authenticity inherent in making a kind of writing they know as readers—a picture book—is hugely significant.

Picture Books Expand Avenues for Meaning Making

Another reason children are encouraged to make picture books is because, in this multimodal publishing format, the weight of meaning is carried as much by illustrations as by words, and readers often extend meanings in significant ways by talking about what they see illustrated in books. Clearly, as explained earlier, writers who are three and four need a variety of ways to capture their thinking, and a picture-book format offers that.

By using both art and writing to compose texts, children extend what they are able to do and learn about communication and composition. In her study of three- and four-year-old writers, Rowe (1994) found that children used the same approach to learn about writing as they did to learn about art. "Because communication was a multimodal event in (and out of) this classroom, children built literacy knowledge that connected art and writing in complex ways" (205). The format of picture books just makes so much more possible for young children who are learning to compose.

Related to this, professional authors and illustrators use the picture-book format as a container for all kinds of writing. When children are helped to see this, they learn to use picture books to compose in a variety of genres. They may make books that tell everyday stories, as Jeffrey did with his book about his dog, or they may make books that are pure fantasy, tell all about something, explain how something is done, or have poems in them. As a publishing container, the possibilities for picture books are really endless.

Making Picture Books Forces the Issue of Composition

Another reason to encourage picture book-making is because the multiple pages of a book force the issue of composition in a way a single page or a journal does not. If there are multiple pages, then what the child is writing about must extend to another page and then another, stretching out in a compositional line, each idea connecting to the one before it in a meaningful way. In other words, the paper that is stapled together is really a metaphor for the whole act of composition. This idea seems simple enough, but it's actually a bit complex. Paper matters.

If a child has just a single piece of paper on which to draw and write, then all the meaning will necessarily be contained on that one page; in and of itself that is not an issue because a single illustration can certainly hold lots and lots of meaning. The issue is that the options for capturing the meaning in a single illustration don't do much to help children understand composition. If a teacher asks a child to dictate a sentence to go with an illustration and then writes that sentence under the child's drawing, the meaning is *reduced* in such a way that it can't even be called a composition any more. Composing involves putting sentences—ideas—together in ways that make sense. A single sentence doesn't help a child understand that.

The other option for capturing the meaning in the illustration is to allow the child to simply create an oral text for it—to just say it or tell it, in other words.

This option often greatly *expands* the meaning, but at a real cost to understanding composition. Mimicking the dramatic composing they do during their play, many children compose richly complex and lengthy oral texts to match a single illustration on a single page. As long as someone will keep listening, children will keep talking and adding to the oral texts that go with their pictures. When they do this, however, their understanding of what *text is* and its relationship to meaning is limited. If they're just saying more words about the same illustration, they're not developing the same *ordered* sense of composition that children get when the next thing that happens, or is revealed, is pictured on the next page and the next.

When composing on the multiple pages of picture books, children come to understand that new pages with new illustrations and words on them are what extend the meaning, nurturing a significantly more sophisticated understanding of expanding text and its relationship to meaning. Consider, for example, the book in Figure 2.4 about Snow White written by Matt's three-year-old daughter Molly, a little girl who loves the whole idea of Snow White. Each new page brings a new activity for Snow White, carefully rendered in the illustrations.

Now here's where all this gets a little complicated. As contradictory as it might seem, when children compose texts orally across multiple pages and illustrations, they often create somewhat more contained narratives or listing texts than they would if they were composing texts orally from single illustrations. There are more pages, but fewer words to go with them. When they read their books, the understanding that they must turn the page and say the next part that goes with the illustration often keeps children from going off on tangents and making up fascinatingly endless text. The pages of the book act as boundaries, in other words, to rein in the oral text in a way a single page usually doesn't.

Imagine that Molly, having no need to follow the symbolic boundaries created by the pages in her Snow White book, was instead composing a story for Snow White to match a single picture she'd drawn of the princess. She would almost certainly compose a fuller, more fanciful text than the one she read and reread in the book. So the question arises, "Which is a more valuable literacy engagement for her?" If all the text she composes is going to be oral anyway, would it be better for that text to be more complex but less connected to symbolic representations (her successive illustrations across pages)? Or would it be better to have Molly compose a *less* sophisticated text so that she gains a *more* sophisticated understanding of how symbols should carry the meaning in written texts?

Teachers who have children make picture books are perhaps choosing to give up a bit of something (richer composition) to get something else (deeper understandings about writing) and have decided the trade-off is worth it. After all, it's not a complete trade-off anyway. For one thing, many young writers go right

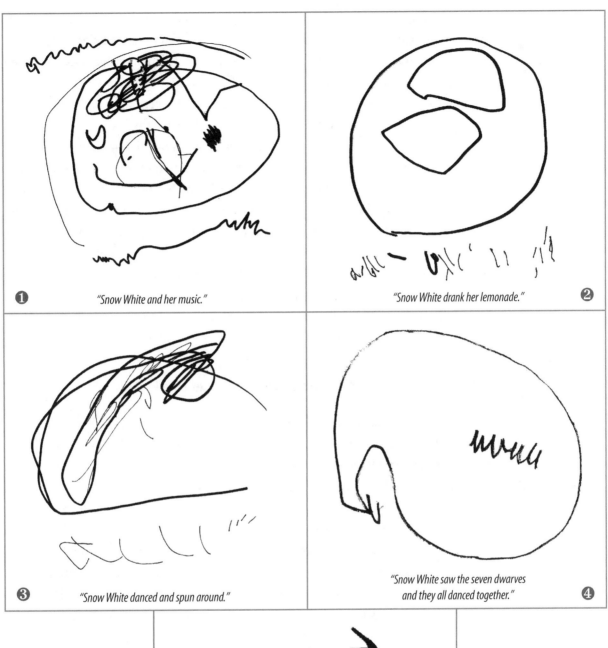

① "Snow White and her music."

② "Snow White drank her lemonade."

③ "Snow White danced and spun around."

④ "Snow White saw the seven dwarves and they all danced together."

⑤

FIG. 2.4 *Molly's Book About Snow White*

ahead and compose some fairly elaborate texts that stretch across the pages in their picture books. For another thing, most days in preschool classrooms afford children multiple opportunities to use all sorts of rich language outside of their writing. Dramatic play, for instance, often involves children weaving rich narratives to guide the action. Similarly, most preschoolers' independent reading is actually a storytelling event, the children drawing the narrative either from memory or from looking at the illustrations in an unfamiliar book.

The thing is, as long as children are having rich oral language experiences across the day, then there are no worries if the act of composing in a picture book reins in their talk a bit. It should rein it in. As a matter of fact, it's useful to understand that composing reins in even the most proficient writer's talk to a great extent. A person can go on and on with talk with an ease he won't find when trying to write it all down and have it hold its meaning without being there. Oral language and written language carry very different potentials actually, and the texts children compose that run across the multiple pages of picture books help them begin to understand these different potentials.

Making Picture Books Helps Children Read Like Writers

As children make picture books, they develop an "insider stance" when it comes to looking at picture books, and this stance is what helps them read like writers (Smith 1988; Ray 1999). What does it mean to read like a writer? As Katie and Lisa Cleaveland explain in *About the Authors* (2004):

> Reading like a writer means that when you read, you think about more than just what a text is about, its meaning. When you read like a writer, you also notice and think about *how* a text is written, because you write yourself and you just notice things like that. People who cook a lot notice things about food that people who don't cook don't notice. People who garden notice things about plants, people who play music notice things about music, and people who write notice things about how texts are written. They can't help it; who they are determines how they see the world. So when children come to think about themselves as people who make books, they begin to look at books differently. Everything they notice about how books are made becomes something they might try when they make them. (14–15)

In preschool classrooms where children regularly make picture books, teachers embed so much of their teaching support for this writing in the talk they have around read-alouds. Every time a book is shared, there is an opportunity to notice what authors and illustrators are doing in books, and then to turn that noticing into an invitation, "Hey, somebody in here could try this in one of their books." But the invitation only makes sense if children are doing the same kind of writing and illustrating on their own that they see others do in the books they read. Since the reading diet of most preschoolers is one of picture books, it makes sense that this is the kind of text they should be making. In Chapters 7 and 8 you'll read lots more about how teachers support young children to develop an insider stance and learn to write well from their reading.

Making Picture Books Builds Stamina

Without a doubt, one thing all competent writers have in common is that they have developed stamina for the task of writing. The first rule of writing well is learning to sit down and stay there for a long time. Things don't get written—well or otherwise—if that first rule isn't followed. And more often than not, the stamina of one sitting is not even enough. A writer has to be willing to come back the next day, sit down again (with the same piece of writing), and stay there for a long time.

Knowing how important stamina is to becoming competent at writing, it's difficult to imagine nurturing writers at any age without also thinking about encouraging their stamina. Of course, children who are three and four aren't known for possessing great stamina, but many of them do show a willingness to stay with something if it's engaging for them. The picture-book format, with its multiple pages waiting to be filled, encourages children to stay at the task of writing for a while—a three- and-four-year-old while, for sure, but a while nonetheless. Occasionally, some of them will even come back to the same book on another day, experiencing a little of what it's like to have stamina over time as well as in one sitting. The making of picture books is, at the very least, a good lunge in the right direction in terms of developing very young children's stamina for writing.

Making Picture Books Is Fun. Children Like It

Actually, "it's fun" and "they like it" are not good reasons to justify an educational practice. Children think lots of things are fun that aren't necessarily good for them educationally, and entertaining three- and four-year-olds is not the same as educating them. Having said all that, most preschoolers think making books is fun. They like it. This makes their teachers happy too, not that this is a good educational goal either.

In all seriousness, if children who are making books aren't enjoying themselves, something is amiss. As explained in Chapter 1, writing should provide children with an invitation, not an expectation, and when children choose to make books, they do so because the idea of making them seems inviting to them. Whatever they're doing as they make books is clearly developmentally appropriate for them because they initiated it. It's happy work, and it actually looks and sounds a whole lot like the happy work children do as they build with blocks or sculpt with clay or make jewelry from beads. Children like to make things, and so the idea of *making* a picture book is very inviting.

Almost the only time it ever gets unhappy is when adults show up bringing too many expectations with them. Of course, adults need to show up alongside children who are making books, helping them do things that are just a little beyond what they can do all on their own (Vygostky 1978). But it's tricky business because the line between "I can do this" and "I'm way too frustrated by what you're suggesting" is a thin one indeed. Later in this book, we address in depth how adults work with young writers to nudge their development and keep everyone happy. The bottom line is that making picture books should be fun for children and they should like it, because if they do, that's the best indicator a teacher has that the task is developmentally appropriate.

To summarize: making picture books makes sense as project writing for young children for several reasons. Picture books:

- are a familiar kind of writing.

- expand avenues for meaning-making.

Making picture books:

- forces the issue of composition (because of multiple pages).

- helps children read like writers.

- builds stamina for writing.

- is fun and children like it.

As stated earlier, in Jeffrey's classroom, his teachers privilege and encourage book-making as a literacy experience because it requires the thinking process of composition, and they've made time, space, and materials available so that children can choose to make books whenever they like. Let's briefly consider the simple issues of time, space, and materials to support this work, then, in the chapters that follow, look at the more complex issues of teachers privileging and encouraging book-making as a literacy experience.

Time, Space, and Materials

Making books is a project children choose to do in preschool classrooms, and they are free to make this choice on most any ordinary day. Virtually any time they're not taking part in some group activity, children may choose to make books, and they can spend as much or as little time engaged with it as they like. Sometimes when children are making books, an adult will be there interacting with them, but sometimes that won't be the case. Children are welcome to make books all on their own or with other children if adults are busy doing other things.

In terms of space, most teachers find it helpful to have a central location where children go if they want to make books. A table where three to five children can sit beside one another is ideal. There won't always be that many children there, but sometimes there may be more children wanting to write than available space. If that happens, writers can either come back later or find another spot in the room where they can write.

The supplies for making books should be kept very simple. Children will need either prestapled blank books (three to four sheets folded), or paper and a stapler so that they can make the books themselves, and markers, pencils, and crayons. You might consider having laminated alphabet charts available (with picture representations of key sound words on them) at the tables where children write; keep in mind, however, that many three- and four-year-old writers won't be ready to use charts to help them spell for quite some time. The charts will be useful though for children who want to make letters to help them remember what the different symbols look like.

In truth, there is nothing really magical about the time, space, and materials needed to have children making books in preschool. Most classrooms have all the supplies, and many have a place for writing set up already. What's magical is the privileging and encouraging that can be done to support young children's sense of selves as writers alongside all their book-making, and how teachers can nudge young writers' development in remarkable ways. Of course, it's not really *magical* teaching either. It's a deeply intellectual and theoretical endeavor—this teaching that's happening in Jeffrey's classroom—and the next chapters consider how it all comes to be.

Meet Isabella

Author and Illustrator of What Princesses Eat

Like many preschool children, Isabella loves princesses. She loves talking about princesses, playing princesses, and, of course, writing about princesses. Many of the books Isabella wrote early in the year were stories about princesses and their many adventures.

Later in the year, Isabella saw many of her friends write and share books that didn't tell stories. Instead, the books fulfilled a different purpose—they taught readers about something or taught readers how to do something. In her preschool class, such books are called "teaching books."

One day, when asked what *kind* of book she was going to make that day, Isabella replied, "A teaching book."

"Really, what is your book going to teach people?"

No one was surprised when Isabella's response was "princesses." The explanation that followed this response was not only surprising, but it also showed just how much she had learned about different types of books. Isabella explained that one page was going to be about what princesses eat, another page would be about what princesses hold, and another would be about what princesses wear. At first she wasn't sure what the fourth page would be, but as you can see, she decided to teach readers how princesses get around.

Isabella held on to her beloved topic, but because of the demonstrations of her writing friends, she wrote with a new vision for what was possible with this topic. Besides what her book teaches readers about princesses (did *you* know princesses drink juice?), *What Princesses Eat* clearly shows that Isabella understands something about genre—how a writer's purpose causes a book to look and sound a certain way.

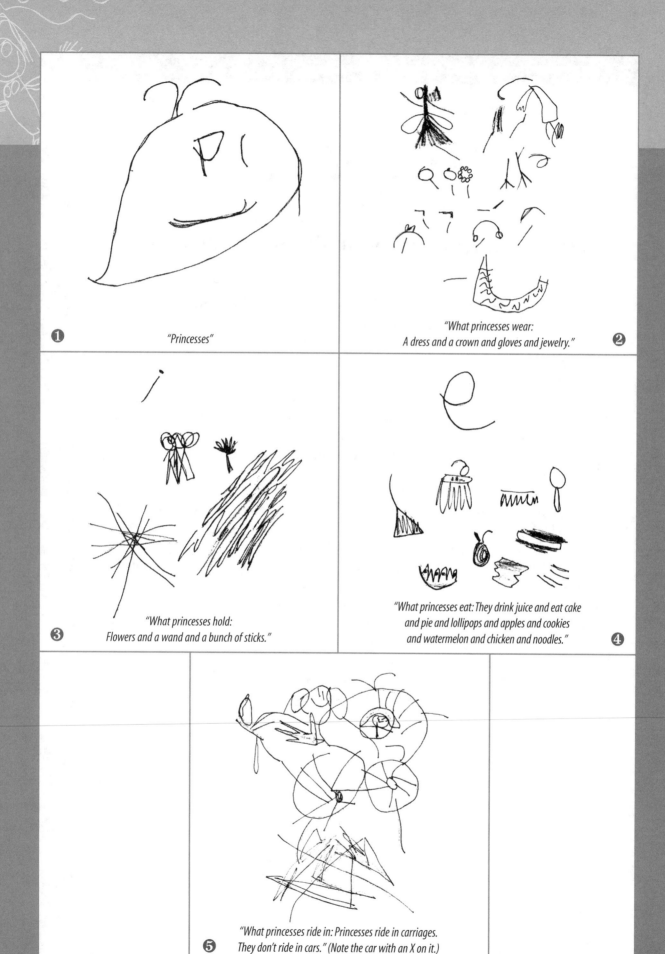

① "Princesses"

② "What princesses wear:
A dress and a crown and gloves and jewelry."

③ "What princesses hold:
Flowers and a wand and a bunch of sticks."

④ "What princesses eat: They drink juice and eat cake
and pie and lollipops and apples and cookies
and watermelon and chicken and noodles."

⑤ "What princesses ride in: Princesses ride in carriages.
They don't ride in cars." (Note the car with an X on it.)

FIG. 2.5 *Isabella's Book About Princesses*

Rethinking the Meaning of Writing Development

For quite a while one afternoon, Shayna sits next to Colin at a table and works on a book about herself and her friends. Colin is working with Matt, and while she can hear them, Shayna doesn't seem distracted by them. She works on her book quite independently, interjecting only once in response to Colin saying, "I don't know how to make a TV." She quickly offers to show him how and draws a huge TV on the back of one of the pages of her book. They look at it together, and then both go back to working on their own books.

After a few minutes, Matt sits beside Shayna and asks her to read her book to him. At first she says she doesn't know how to read it, but Matt explains, "It's like pretending if you did have words there, what would they say?" At this, Shayna takes her finger and moves it along the lines of writing in her book and begins to read. As she reads, Matt restates and clarifies what she's saying on each page, helping Shayna grab hold of her meaning. They don't get very far with the reading, though, because she can't help but get very involved in thinking like a writer. Shayna keeps stopping to engage in the back-and-forth, recursive process of drafting and revising her text.

Matt learned so much about Shayna as a writer from interacting with her around this book. To understand some of what he learned, first take a look at the completely finished text (Figure 3.1), and then we'll go back in time and explain how *Shayna and Her Friends* came to be.

The idea for this book seemed to come from an experience Shayna had and she was quite intentional in her efforts to faithfully record it as it happened. Matt learned this when Shayna corrected his reading of the first page after he reversed the names of the two friends. "No, *Naomi* saw *Lilly*," she said. Trying to repeat her reading to her, Matt had incorrectly said it the other way around.

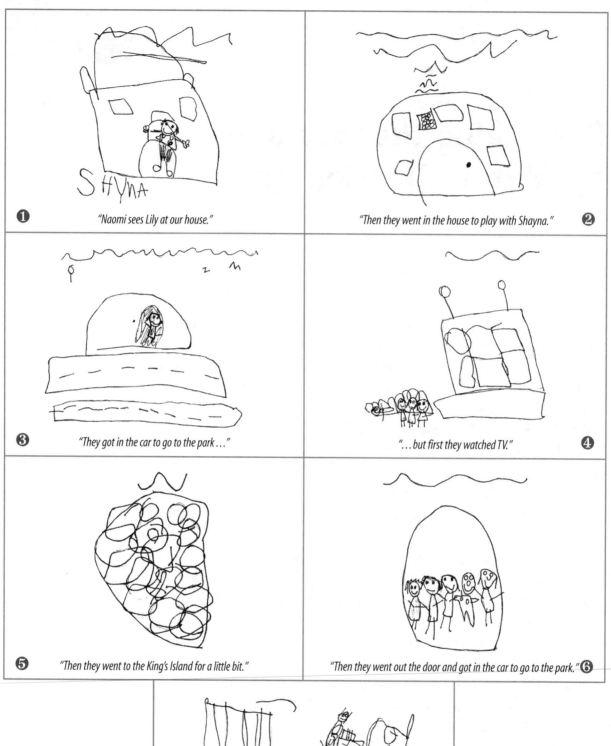

❶ *"Naomi sees Lily at our house."*

❷ *"Then they went in the house to play with Shayna."*

❸ *"They got in the car to go to the park …"*

❹ *"… but first they watched TV."*

❺ *"Then they went to the King's Island for a little bit."*

❻ *"Then they went out the door and got in the car to go to the park."*

❼ *"They are playing at the park. They went on the swings and slide. They all bumped together."*

FIG. 3.1 **Shayna's Book—Shayna and Her Friends**

Shayna corrected Matt's reading again on the second page when he read, "They went in the house to play with me." "Not with *me*, with *Shayna*," she said. This correction seems indicative of two things. One was her intention, again, for this book to faithfully recount what happened. She had actually said *me* when she first read this page to Matt, but his saying it likely confused her because *he* was not the correct *me* in the narrative. She wanted to be clear that it was her, Shayna. Both the first- and second-page corrections to Matt's reading show that she clearly understands her position as the book's author. Shayna is in charge of what it says and how it says it. She also pointed out the friends playing together in the upstairs window, indicating intentional decision making in her illustrations as well.

On page three, Shayna revised to make her meaning clearer after she read this page to Matt. Looking at the illustration, she realized that Lilly was pictured in the car but that the door was still open. Shayna scribbled over Lilly to show that the door was closed, and then added a tiny dot to the left side when Colin (still sitting next to her) reminded her she needed to lock the door. This entire act of revision was completely unprompted, showing that Shayna understood and engaged independently in the recursive process of revision to make her meaning clearer.

After closing and locking the door of the car, Shayna started to read the next page and was immediately stumped because she realized she and her friends were supposed to be going to the park. That's what she'd said when she read the previous page, "They are in the car and going to the park." But what she saw on page four was not the park, but the TV she'd drawn to show Colin how to make one. "Oh no. I forgot about the park," she said. Matt sensed her frustration and suggested she add a piece of paper to the book so that she could add the park page. But Shayna didn't want to do that. Instead, she wanted to add a page to the very end of the book, which she began doing immediately, asserting her willfulness as an author over the decision-making process. So to be clear, understand that the park page you see at the end in Figure 3.1 did not exist when Shayna first said she was finished with this book and began sharing it with Matt.

When Shayna finished adding the park page, Matt asked her whether she could start from the beginning and read the book all the way through. Remember they had never gotten past the words for page three the first time because Shayna insisted on revising as soon as she realized she'd forgotten the park. On the second reading, Shayna smartly incorporated language into her reading that helped account for the park page she'd added and its place in the narrative. Page three still reads as it did originally: "They got in the car to go to the park"; but when she turns to read page four, Shayna says, "But first they watched TV." Beginning the text on this page with the conjunction *but* shows that Shayna understands the need to mark the relationship between the ideas she's composing.

Related to this, Matt learned that when Shayna first drew the illustration on page six, the original ending for the book, her intention was to show the girls going home from King's Island in the car. But after the addition of the park page—the new ending—Shayna read page six as "They got in the car and went to the park." Again, this showed she understood that when she writes, the ideas are supposed to connect in meaningful ways.

Looking Beyond the Artifact

If we had a dollar for every time we've shared a young child's writing, such as Shayna's, and said some version of, "You should have been there," we'd be wealthy folks. The pieces of paper themselves just never tell the story, and they certainly never do the children justice as writers. In this chapter, we'd like to think about that, about doing children justice as writers, and how essential this justice is to nurturing their development.

If you just look at the book Shayna made on this afternoon, and the words she composed to go with it, there is no way to see the amazing thinking she engaged in as she composed *Shayna and Her Friends*. This is in fact true of every writing artifact in the world. The book you're reading, for example, is a writing artifact and is the result of thousands of decisions made about every word, sentence, paragraph, and chapter along the way. Things were changed, moved, added in, taken out and completely scrapped, and yet you—the reader—see none of that; you see only the end result. Of course, as long as you're only interested in this book as a reader, then the end result is your only interest.

Teachers, however, are not solely interested in the end result of children's writing. They cannot be. Teachers must be interested in how children's writing comes to be, and nowhere is this more important than in teaching the very youngest writers like Shayna. To even begin to understand her development as a writer, a teacher must be present with Shayna and the book she has made, and that teacher must listen and watch closely as this young writer reveals the complex thinking she is doing while composing. All of it, by the way, is *exactly the same kind of thinking* we engaged in as we wrote the book you're now reading.

The importance of this understanding cannot be overstated. Young writers engage in all the same kinds of thinking most proficient writers engage in as they write, but their thinking is often overlooked, or not taken seriously, because their writing is not yet representational in a conventional sense. By *representational* we mean "able to hold its meaning on its own without the writer there." In Shayna's case, her illustrations represent her meanings quite well, particularly once you know the text that accompanies them, but the text itself, other than her name, cannot represent her meaning without her there to read it. If the adults in her life don't acknowledge her writing simply because it's not yet representational, then they never even see the amazing thinking about writing she is clearly capable of doing.

In their study of the literacy development of young children documented in the hugely important book, *Language Stories and Literacy Lessons*, Harste, Woodward, and Burke (1984) made this exact same argument more than twenty years ago. They put it this way:

> For many adults, literacy means to represent the world on their terms, with their templates . . . [but] the young child is a written language user long before his writing looks representational . . . [and] the decisions which the young child makes are, both in form and in kind, like those which we make as literate adults. When we confuse product with process, we fail to note the onset of literacy and, in so doing, also fail to appreciate the real literacy achievement made by 3-year-olds. (16)

For him to learn so much about her as a writer, indeed to appreciate her real literacy achievement, Matt had to be willing to let Shayna represent her writing to him on her own terms, and then to interact with her as a writer on those terms. He couldn't ask her writing to do more or be more on its own than what she made of it while present. He understood an important point that Harste, Woodward, and Burke go on to make: "In order to judge the quality of a literacy experience one must judge the quality of the mental trip taken, not the arrival point per se" (18). If Matt were only a reader of Shayna's text, then he would be interested only in its "arrival point," the finished product; but as her teacher, he has different reasons for engaging with the text she has composed. As her teacher, he needs to understand the "mental trip taken" so that he can help her along on this journey of writing development on which she's clearly embarked.

All teachers of writing should be interested in the mental trips taken by the writers in their care, whether that writing is representational or not. Lucy Calkins' (1994) sage advice to teach the writer, not the writing, comes directly from this understanding. In truth, once the writing is representational, it sometimes becomes more difficult for teachers to focus on writers because they're so distracted by all the needs they see in the way the writing is transcribed. The beauty of working with the youngest writers is that teachers *have* to focus on them and their thinking because there's not much to see yet on the actual pages. Of course, this beauty is only possible if teachers believe they can nurture children's development as writers before their writing becomes representational—the argument we're making here. Before we move forward with that argument, we need to consider how children's writing becomes representational.

Transcription and Spelling Development

The skill of *transcription* (getting the words down), which we discussed in Chapter 2, is the skill that writers use to make written text representational and able to hold its meaning without them being present. The way writers "get the words down," of course, is by using the spelling system of English to capture each word, and then the conventions of punctuation to show the relationships among words. Developing the skill of accurate transcription takes quite a long time, in large part because of the complexity of the English spelling system, which is only partially alphabetic. Sandra Wilde (1992) points out seven features of the system that, when taken together, make it so complex.

1. We don't have enough letters (26 of them, and about 40 sounds, depending on dialect).

2. Spellings vary according to a sound's position in the word and are affected by other letters in the word.

3. We have some arbitrary rules that aren't even directly connected to pronunciation.

4. Spelling reflects meaning as well as pronunciation.

5. English has words adopted from other languages.

6. Oral language changes more over time than spelling does.

7. Spoken dialects differ more than spelling does. (15–16)

Despite this complexity, the vast majority of people do manage to eventually gain control of the spelling system. Several decades of solid research have documented the fairly predictable ways children gradually develop competence in transcription with lots of experience writing and reading (Bissex 1980; Clay 1975; Dyson 1993; Ferreiro and Teberosky 1982; Gentry and Gillet 1993; Henderson and Beers 1980; Read 1971; Schickendanz 1999; Sulzby 1989; Sulzby and Teale 1985). These different predictable ways writers represent meaning as they develop the skill of transcription are no doubt familiar to any-one who spends much time around young children, and they are also already well documented in the professional literature devoted to early literacy. So, per-haps at the risk of oversimplifying, we'd like to offer just a brief review of typi-cal development in transcription, and then we'll move on to considering the impact of this development on nurturing young children as writers.

The very first representations that children make are usually with drawings, and often these drawings require children to be present to share their expressed meaning (Figure 3.2). At some point most children begin to add marks that are linear in nature to these drawings. These marks are distinguished from the draw-ings by their linearity and directionality, showing the features of written English. Some people refer to this as *scribble writing* (Figure 3.3), although researchers have found (Harste et al. 1984) that the marks are usually made with some intention in mind and only appear as random scribbles (33). Over time, the scribbles will come to resemble more closely the actual letters of the alphabet. They'll be almost letters, but not quite (Figure 3.4).

Learning to make the letters in one's name actually propels many children to start using the letters of the alphabet in their writing (often alongside made-up symbols for letters), and at this point, most children will use them in random strings to represent their meanings (Figure 3.5). The more letters children

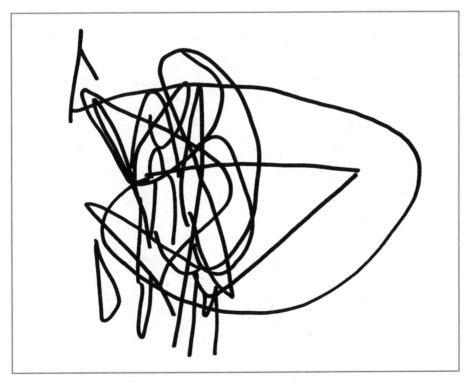

FIG. 3.2 *Drawing as Representation*

FIG. 3.3   *Scribble Writing*

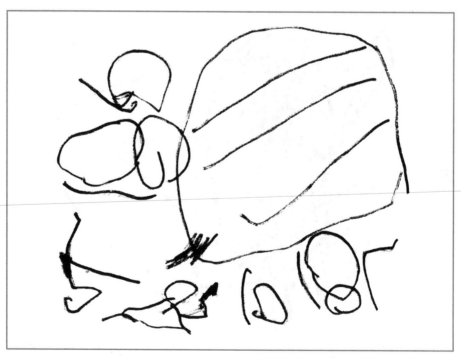

FIG. 3.4   *Mock Letters*

FIG. 3.5 *Random Strings of Letters*

remember, the more variety they'll have in their random strings. Around this time, many children also begin remembering what certain words look like, particularly words in their environment, so it's not uncommon for a sight word to show up among all the random strings of letters. Sometimes the sight word is there to represent its shared meaning, and sometimes not; it's just there because it looks like a word.

Eventually children will begin to use what many refer to as *invented spelling* to represent their meanings. Invented spelling involves children being intentional about *which* letters they are using to represent words for the first time. Young writers' intentionality comes from their growing knowledge base about how spellings come to be, so a wide range of development can be seen in invented spellings. As children invent spellings, they sometimes begin by using single letters to represent whole words and will almost always hear and write consonant sounds before vowel sounds (Figure 3.6). But over time most of them begin to use very sophisticated spellings that aren't yet conventional but show a rich knowledge base of letter–sound relationships, visual memory, meanings, and word lengths (Figure 3.7).

FIG. 3.6 *Invented Spelling: "Car"*

FIG. 3.7 *Invented Spelling: "Macaroni and Cheese"*

By using various forms of invented spellings, for the first time children experience what it is like for texts to hold their meanings when they aren't present. This experience can be both empowering and frustrating for them. It's empowering because children know that their writing is now working more like adult writing. But it can be frustrating because now their own texts present them with expectations for reading them "right." Many young children who use invented spelling to capture their extensive oral vocabularies actually "outwrite" themselves as readers and have a difficult time reading what they've written.

Related to this, children using invented spelling generally understand that the words they say when they read must match their written words, so for quite some time they compose much simpler books than the ones they did when no word-to-word matches were necessary. Adults need to understand the mixed feelings that children often have about this aspect of their development.

Finally, as children gain experience writing and reading (where they see so many words in print), they will begin to use more and more conventional spellings as they remember them and make them part of the repertoire of words they know how to spell. Accurate transcription becomes possible, not because writers never encounter another word they don't know how to spell, but because they learn to manage spelling as needed in various situations. Writers know when they are unsure of spellings and can decide whether the writing task warrants inventing spellings as placeholders or the need to seek a resource to get the spellings right.

The research around spelling development (cited earlier) clearly shows that children's development doesn't always occur in a linear, sequential fashion as they learn to represent their meanings with words. Interestingly enough, in Shayna's writing you see a good example of this because she uses three different kinds of writing in one book. She uses conventional letters to spell her name, scribble writing across the pages, and a combination of made-up and actual random letters on page three.

Spelling Development Is Not Writing Development

To understand how teachers can nurture children's development as writers before their writing becomes representational, it is essential to understand that transcription is just one of many things a writer needs to know and be able to do in order to make something with writing. As noted in Chapter 2, compositional writing is a recursive process that requires writers to think deeply—about purpose, ideas, organization, word choices, craft, genre, tone, audience, presentation, and so on—and then use the skills of transcription to capture all that thinking on paper or on a computer.

In many ways, transcription is actually the least significant thing a writer learns to do because it's the one writing skill that is well served by technology. Word processors have radically changed the way writers deal with spelling and handwriting—the essential tools of transcription. One of the greatest minds of our time, Stephen Hawking, is in fact unable to transcribe even with a word processor because of physical limitations, yet he manages to be a very prolific and influential writer.

Our point in putting transcription in its place is not to trivialize it in any way or to imply that we don't hope to see young children developing their full potential as writers, including the ability to accurately transcribe their messages. Our point is that development in spelling (transcription) is not the *same thing* as development in writing. Spelling development only represents one trajectory of development necessary to become a competent writer who composes meaningful text. Imagine the implications when a word, such as *precommunicative*, is used to refer to a particular stage of spelling development if adults aren't aware that the word is a label for the symbols the child uses to represent meaning, not the child's thinking process as a writer.

When the well-documented phases of spelling development are considered to be the *same thing* as writing development, the misconception leads to instructional practices that greatly underserve children as writers. An emphasis is placed on transcription at the expense of everything else because development along this trajectory is so discernable. After all, what spelling development *looks* like is so clear.

What writing development looks like beyond transcription, however, is much less clear, in large part because adults have difficulty imagining what the thinking process of writing looks like if it's not connected to actual words on a page.[1] Adults may see Shayna go back and color over Lilly to show the car door is closed and think that this is a smart thing for her to do, but not necessarily understand her action as revision. But in doing this, Shayna has done *exactly* what more proficient writers do when they reread and realize some meaning is not clear. She made it clearer. Once adults understand a move like this as revision, they'll begin noticing that children engage in spontaneous, intentional revision all the time when they're writing, as well as all the other processes writers use as they compose. In fact, at a process level, Harste and his colleagues found "no compelling evidence that the behavior of young readers and writers is a function of different psycholinguistic and sociolinguistic activity" than that of experienced writers (1984, 69).

---

1 Dorn and Saffos (2001) also consider composing separately from transcribing in children's writing development, but not until the onset of representational transcription. Their definition of emergent writers does not include children who are not yet hearing and recording sounds in words (4–9).

To understand how significant Shayna's development as a writer is, consider what just this one artifact of process and product from her writing life shows us about her. As a writer, Shayna

- chose to engage in writing from a variety of other activities she might have chosen.

- selected a topic that was meaningful to her and was from her own experience.

- worked independently over time to compose her text.

- remained focused on her topic throughout her text.

- made clear, logical connections between the ideas in her text.

- offered assistance to another writer.

- engaged in revision, making changes to her book to make her meaning clearer.

- discovered and then solved a problem of some complexity in her writing.

- represented her meanings using both illustrations and print.

- understood and preserved her authority as the author of her book.

- read and reread her book with consistency over time.

- responded to her audience's questions about the book with confidence.

We believe a list like this makes it so clear that spelling development just cannot be considered the same thing as writing development, particularly when the focus is on using writing to compose. Just look at all that is lost if the focus is only on Shayna's ability to transcribe.

More than anything else, training our eyes and ears to notice what the thinking process of writing looks like when it's not connected to words on the page has dramatically shifted our understanding of what young writers do as they compose.[2] We've had to take what we know about the thinking and actions of the most experienced writers and use it as a lens through which to understand writing development in those who have the least experience. Again and again we've asked, "What does it look like when a child who is three or four composes?" And we need to make it very clear that we've worked to understand

---

2 To note this shift in thinking, see Katie's discussion of revision in her book, *About the Authors*, with Lisa Cleaveland (2004, 71–73). It's about revision of *written* text only, a much too narrow definition to be helpful in the work with writers whose texts are not yet representational.

development in just this way: writing as a process enacted by three- and four-year-olds. We've tried to understand development using *their* templates for writing, not our own.

Along the way, we decided to call this development *composition development* instead of *writing development* for a few important reasons. First, as explained in Chapter 2, our primary interest is in what children do when they use writing to compose, when they make something with writing as Shayna made her book.

Second, we know that the act of composing can be—an indeed most often is—a multimodal process. Depending on the potential of the publishing format (picture book, magazine, newspaper, website, blog, etc.), composing a text means combining written words with art, graphics, layout, audio, and even video to achieve the desired effect in a composition. Composing a text is not just about writing words, in other words. Certainly three- and four-year-old writers do combine art with their written texts as they compose. So in truth, writing development by itself is not the focus—the focus is composition development.

Finally, our interest is also in composition as a habit of mind—a natural way of thinking that begins when a person asks, "How might this go?" When Matt's daughter Natalie was three, she and Matt were in the car and he asked her what she was going to put on her page of the scrapbook the children would give to their mother for Mother's Day. Natalie, who makes books and composes often, naturally began thinking in a compositional way. She said she was going to draw herself and her sister and Matt and Bridget, and then at the top of the page (she was very clear about the positioning), she was going to write herself saying, "Thank you Mom." Matt asked how she would write that, and she said, "I'll use a speech bubble." Natalie imagined the entire composition, using illustrations, words, layout, and craft to think out how she might represent her meaning (Figure 3.8).

This kind of thinking—the ability to imagine how it all could go and how it might all come together—is what we think of as a composing habit of mind. It's a forward sort of thinking, and someone like Natalie who engages naturally in such thinking likely has a strong sense of agency because she is able to imagine things into being. So indeed, again, it's not just writing development that interests us, it's whole ways of thinking.

We know that many adults have a less-than-positive history with the word *composition*. As a word used in schools, it refers to a particular kind of writing that no one really wants to do. It never was a good word to use to begin with, because *composition* is not the name of what people write in the world outside of school. You don't go to the bookstore and ask the clerk to help you find some good "compositions" to read.

"Thank you, Mom!"

FIG. 3.8 *A Page Natalie Composed for Mother's Day*

But the bottom line is: When we looked at the definitions for *compose* (cited in Chapter 2), there just wasn't a better word to describe the thinking aspect of writing that so fascinated us as young children made books. So we've stayed with it, keeping writers like Sean and Jeffrey and Shayna in mind, realizing that *composing* is exactly what they are doing as they make books about flamingos and lost dogs and friends going to the park.

The chapters in the second part of this book are devoted to exploring teaching practices that nurture young writers, and without a doubt, rethinking the meaning of writing development in this way—expanding it to include children's growing understandings about composition—has caused us to reconsider so much of this practice. In Chapter 4, we define what we mean by composition development so that an understanding of it can serve as a lens through which the rest of this book can be read.

Meet Regan

Author and Illustrator of Picnic

A sense of energy and excitement is important for any writing, especially in preschool, so teachers watch children and look for opportunities to connect writing with other engagements children enjoy. This sort of teacher watchfulness is what led to Reagan's book, *Picnic*.

One day in February the writing area was taken over with various children's projects, so Matt decided to spend some time in the dramatic play area where McKenzie and Reagan were busy getting ready for a picnic. Reagan quickly pulled Matt into the girls' play by writing down his order for the kind of soup he wanted on the picnic. Matt didn't realize soup was essential picnic food, but since it was "heart soup" they were making, he ordered a bowl to go.

After lots of preparation and warnings to stay on the path to avoid the bears during the hike, the trio reached their picnic destination—a spot on the other side of the room. Nearby, Kyle was playing a tune on a keyboard and was invited to join the picnic. Kyle said he wasn't hungry, but he offered to keep playing while they ate their soup.

At the end of this engaging play experience, Matt told Reagan and McKenzie he'd had a wonderful time. In fact, he had such a wonderful time, he wondered whether the girls might be able to write about the picnic so he could remember it. McKenzie and Reagan literally skipped off to the writing center, got some blank books, and skipped back to the dramatic play area where they started working energetically on their books.

Reagan's book was a departure from the more list-like books she'd made before this day. The narrative structure of the play scenario came easily to her and she worked on the book for quite a while.

The next day as Reagan read her story to a teacher, she realized there were details missing. In the midst of reading, she decided she'd forgotten a page and went off to add the last page you see in Figure 3.9. After adding the page, she started reading again, but again she realized she wanted to revise. This time she went back and added the speech bubbles you see on each page, carefully matching the number of bubbles to what each character was saying.

Reagan's revision process is actually quite typical. Many preschool writers act quickly to revise their illustrations and writing to match the evolving meanings in their books, and talk especially supports this sort of revision. What Reagan's process shows is how dramatic play can support the development of meaning, and particularly the development of narrative. Because Reagan had lived her story first through dramatic play, she was able to develop it more fully as a narrative and to draw from the details she remembered from being actively engaged in the experience.

 "McKenzie is cooking soup."

 "We're going into the woods to eat soup."

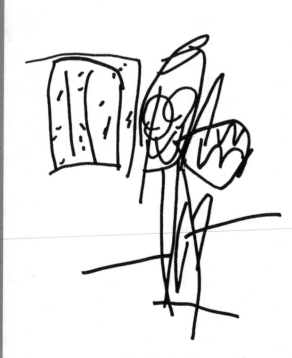

"There is Kyle in the woods.
He is playing piano."

"We are walking back home to play."

FIG. 3.9 **Reagan's Book, Picnic**

Understanding Dimensions of Composition Development

In mid-May, while working together with different children who are making books in a preschool classroom, we're both impressed with how much they have grown and changed as writers over the course of a school year. The writing itself doesn't look that different. The children's books still look like they were made by three- and four-year-olds. It's the writers who look different to us. Training our eyes to see and understand what composition development looks like has helped us see so much more in what children know and are able to do as writers.

So what does composition development look like? The purpose of this chapter is to explore different dimensions of this development within the context of children's composing. Following a belief that assessment should always lead instruction, we've framed the various dimensions of development as questions teachers might ask themselves about the picture books children make and the process they go through as they make them. The questions should lead to observations and interactions that will help teachers understand children's composition development.

You may remember that in Chapter 2 we explained why "making picture books" was a rich template on which children might engage in the thinking process of writing. Because teachers need to ask these questions when children are engaged in compositional writing, each of them is tied to the act of making a picture book. As you read through the questions in the sections that follow and think about the development related to each one, remember that the answers to these questions cannot be found in the books alone. The written products mean very little without the children there to represent them, and some of the questions can only be answered through observation as they are actually writing. If a child has finished a book, the opportunity to understand some dimensions of his or her development has been lost.

We've organized the dimensions of composition development into three broad categories: 1) understandings about texts, 2) understandings about process, and 3) understandings about what it means to be a writer. As with most efforts to categorize, there is some overlap in the various dimensions, but for the most part, they serve an important role in framing composition development in broad strokes rather than narrow ones.

We should add, however, that as best we understand it, composition development is always multidimensional and simply refuses to follow lines of logical progression, so the three dimensions are not hierarchical in any way in terms of when or how children develop these understandings. We've simply chosen to consider understandings about texts first because we needed somewhere to start. Likewise, the separate dimensions considered in each category are not ordered in any way.

Understandings About Texts

- Is the child's book *about* something?

- How has the child organized the book? Does it move through time (narrative) or through a list of ideas (non-narrative)?

- When the child reads it, does it sound like a book?

- Does the child read the book basically the same way every time?

- Is the book being made *in the manner* of other picture books?

- What in the book shows the child understands genre?

- How is the child representing meaning?

All the lines of thinking represented by these questions are designed to trace children's growing understandings about written texts—what they are and how they work. It probably goes without saying why writers need to understand so much about texts, but just to say it anyway: Texts are what writers *make* with writing. It's difficult to make something if you don't know anything about what it is you are trying to make. Throughout their lives, writers must continue to update their knowledge about what texts are and how they work every time they encounter new styles, genres, and formats for publishing. A picture book—what young writers are making—is just one kind of text, but the understandings they develop while making them can be generalized to all kinds of texts, so we'll use these terms interchangeably throughout this discussion.

Is the child's book about something?

This question gets at perhaps the most basic of all understanding about texts: that they are focused and should be *about* something. Proficient writers have no doubt understood this about texts for most of their literate lives, but interestingly enough, the understanding should not be taken for granted because it drives so much of a writer's decision making when composing. Why? Because knowing a text should be focused and keeping it that way are entirely two different matters.

When children first start making books, they may not yet understand this about texts. When this is the case, each page of a book will likely be about something different. The book you see in Figure 4.1 is a good example of this. The writer made a book with each page representing something she can draw,

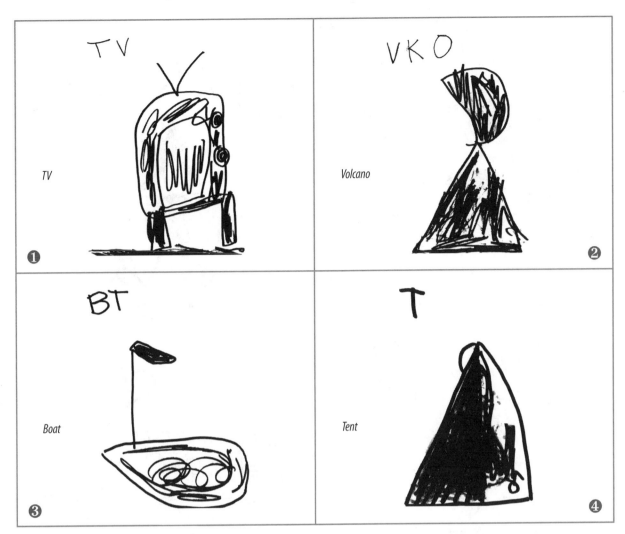

FIG. 4.1 **A Book with No Real Focus**

and as she read it, it was clear there really wasn't a focus beyond this that made the ideas in the book connect in a meaningful way.

What's particularly interesting about this example is that it was done by a child who is moving right along in her spelling development. As you can see on each page, she is already hearing sounds in words and matching them to letters that make those sounds. If transcription is the only focus of her teacher's writing instruction, then there is no reason to nudge her writing development along by teaching her that books are focused and should be about something, and what an opportunity that would be to miss.

There are some other typical kinds of development we've seen as children grow into the understanding that texts are focused. Sometimes the book will be all about something, but in a very loosely connected way, as if the previous writer had said her book was about "things she likes," for example. Sometimes a writer will start out focused on a topic but lose that focus along the way (Figure 4.2). The developmental goal here is for children's books to become

❶ "This is me and my grandma and Clifford."

❷ "This is my mom."

❸ "This is my mom in a bathing suit when she was little."

❹ "Rocketship."

❺ "A house. Clifford."

❻ "Dad, Anna, Clifford, Mom."

FIG. 4.2 *A Book That Loses Focus Along the Way*

"This is my baby brother." ①

"My brother is crying." ②

"Then he was happy." ③

FIG. 4.3 *A Book That Is Less Representational, But More Focused*

more and more focused over time, and for the connections between their ideas to become stronger and more meaningful—the focus of the next dimension of development.

How has the child organized the book?

In other words, does the book move through time (narrative) or through a list of ideas (nonnarrative)? Across the multiple pages of a picture book, each page's ideas should connect somehow as the writer moves forward (once the writer understands the book should be about something). In essence, writers can move forward and connect ideas in one of two ways. They can use a narrative structure and move the ideas through time, telling what happened next and then next. Sean's book about the flamingo who ate too many termites is organized this way (see Chapter 1), and so is Jeffrey's book about his dog Pepper (see Chapter 2). Or writers can move through a list of ideas about something and connect them in some logical way (how the book you're reading is organized). This book about a young writer's family is organized this way (Figure 4.4).

❶ *"Dad, Bryn, Alex."*

❷ *"This is my dad. He is working outside."*

❸ *"This is my sister. She is playing outside."*

❹ *"This is me and my brother. It is raining."*

FIG. 4.4 *A List Book About a Family*

Once a writer has decided whether his basic organization will be a narrative or a nonnarrative, then he'll go on to make all sorts of decisions about exactly how to move through time or how to move through a list. The ability to make more specific and good decisions about organization requires lots and lots of writing experience. Proficient writers certainly compose with an overall sense of organization guiding them, and inexperienced writers can develop the ability to compose in this same way over time.

Before children develop this understanding, you'll often see them mix the kinds of connections they're making between ideas—composing a text that sort of moves through time and sort of moves through a list. The book you see in Figure 4.5 is an example of writing like this.

This book about the zoo moves through time in a way, but that movement is not really significant to the unfolding events. Basically the writer is listing things she did at the zoo, something that is very typical of many children's first narratives; they're very list-like. At the end of the book, the writer seems to lose her narrative thread, reading this page more as a label of the picture than as the next thing that happened, though the focus is maintained.

The developmental goal (that will come with years of experience) is for writers to recognize the organization of their texts and keep it consistent across whole texts. To talk with young children about organization in writing, teachers might use the simple terms *story* (narrative) and *list* (nonnarrative) to refer to the two basic types of texts. As children mature as readers and writers, these terms will necessarily become complicated as their meanings become more nuanced, but they seem to be useful starting words to help them understand the complex issue of organization.

When the child reads it, does it sound like a book?

The sort of crafted language you find in picture books is not just talk written down and it doesn't sound like it is. When proficient writers compose texts, they are careful to craft their writing so it sounds like the kind of writing they're making. Most children will have to grow to understand this, so when first asked to read their books they might simply label the pictures, or they might talk *about* what's in the pictures. Growth in this area is evident when these readings sound more and more like the language found in picture books—the kind of writing the children are making. The three books in Figures 4.6 through 4.8 show a range of development in this dimension, as well as a range of development in terms of the two previous dimensions.

You will probably see that narrative texts are the first to sound the most like actual books when children read them because story language has a particular sound that is familiar to many children. Reading richly crafted nonnarrative

① *Olivia 4*

② *"Me and Alex went to the zoo."*

③ *"We saw a flower and picked it."*

④ *"I saw a cheetah that had orange spots and was purple."*

⑤ *"I saw a butterfly and caught it with a net."*

⑥ *"This is a puffin."*

FIG. 4.5 **A Book with Different Connections Between Ideas**

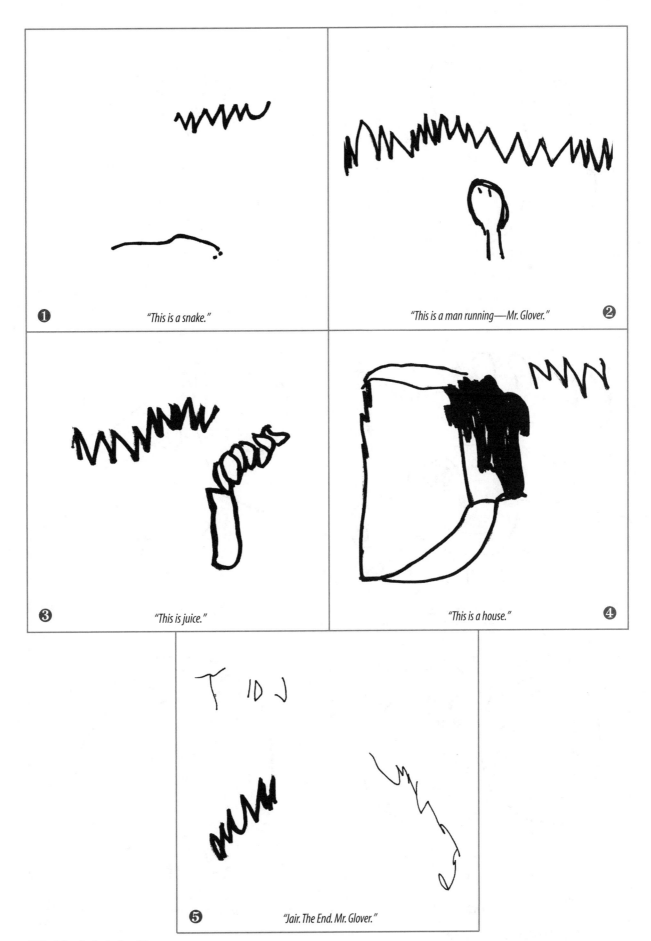

1 "This is a snake."

2 "This is a man running—Mr. Glover."

3 "This is juice."

4 "This is a house."

5 "Jair. The End. Mr. Glover."

FIG. 4.6 *Labels for Pictures*

① Kennedy

② "This is my dad. We're going trick-or-treating."

③ "This is me trick-or-treating."

④ "This is my friend Spikey."

⑤ "These are my brothers."

⑥ "This is Spikey yelling 'Aggghhh!'"

FIG. 4.7 *Labels with Some Details*

"Once there was a land of squiggles and someone went there and looked for a place to sleep."

"And there was somebody there and he was lost. So he stayed there."

"The next morning he got up and went home."

FIG. 4.8 *Sounds More Like the Language of Books*

books to children can help them begin to understand the sound of this less familiar kind of writing.

You might also notice whether having written text in their books, even in its most beginning, scribble-like stages, causes children to read what they've written in ways that sound more like books. We have noticed that, for some children, the presence of any form of written text in conjunction with illustrations causes them to read their texts so that they sound more like books. The presence of print seems to cue children to read differently than when they are reading only from their illustrations.

Does the child read the book basically the same way every time?

This question gets at an understanding that is in fact as much about reading as it is about writing, but it serves both equally and critically. Inexperienced writers will grow to understand that what they represent on each page holds the meaning and that this meaning, unless intentionally revised, should stay constant over time. Proficient writers understand this, of course; that's why they choose to represent their meanings with written words, because that's what written words do—they stay the same. But we know that long before there are written words, there is meaning in a book, so helping them understand that meaning should stay the same over time is helping children understand a very important thing about writing.

As children grow into this understanding, their development will range from reading their books quite differently every time, as if they are making each page up anew; to reading parts of books the same way each time, but not all of them, to a point where their reading stays basically the same over time (in terms of meaning, not necessarily exact words). Growth in this area is also related, of course, to children's drawings becoming more representational and able to hold their meanings more efficiently, as well as to the onset of invented spelling.[1]

Is the book being made in the manner of other picture books?

Proficient writers generally compose with a publishing format (magazine, newspaper, webpage, professional journal, chapter book, picture book, etc.) in mind, and they are always mindful of how the features of that format will impact their final product. Different formats have clearly different potentials for meaning-making—audiovisual potential, graphics, layout, more formal and less formal language expectations, even length impacts the decisions writers make.

When young children add features, such as titles, bylines, dedications, fly pages, tables of contents, and the like, to their books, they are showing a developing understanding that particular formats for publishing (in this case, a picture book) share distinct features. This is an understanding that will serve them well as writers as they eventually move out of picture books and into other publishing formats. Most young writers will begin combining illustrations and some kind of print in their picture books fairly quickly; more advanced development in this area is when you see the child adding other distinct features of picture books as a young writer did for the one shown in Figure 4.9.

The day this book was written, the teacher read the children a nonfiction book about worms that had a "Words You Know" page spread at the end of the

---

1 For more on how children develop an understanding of constancy of message over time in reading, see Elizabeth Sulzby's work (1989) on emergent storybook reading.

❶ *"A cupcake factory"*	*"Elliana"* ❷
❸ *"Ms. Brenda"*	*"My brother Kaleb"* ❹
❺ *"My mom"*	*"My house"* ❻
❼ *"Our school"*	*"And these are all the things you just read about."* ❽

FIG. 4.9 **Family Book with "Words You Know" Boxes at the End**

book. With a boxed photograph accompanying each one, it contained terms such as *roundworms*, *wormcasts*, *burrow*, and *night crawlers*—all of which were featured in the book. Later, when this young writer made a book about his family, on his own he decided to add a page like this to it, with little boxes showing the people and places he'd featured in his book.

What in the book shows the child understands genre?

Genre refers to the various kinds of writing in the world that are written for different purposes and audiences: essays, feature articles, realistic fiction, memoir, interviews, textbook chapters, and so on. Understandings about genre are essential to good writing because they give writers vision for writing; genre is the writer's sense of what he is making with writing (Ray 2006). Children's first sense of what they're making with writing—picture books—doesn't really represent a sense of genre. A picture book is a publishing format, and all kinds of writing can be found in that format.

When young writers begin talking about making *particular kinds* of picture books, then they have begun to develop a sense of genre and are figuring out there are different kinds of writing in the world. This first sense of genre children develop will likely be quite broad and connected to the kinds of topics they're writing about: "This is a funny book about my sister" or "This is a made-up book about a flamingo." But as they are exposed to the idea of genre when teachers share books with them, they'll broaden the repertoire of possibilities for genre, and may write all kinds of things: informational books about topics of interest, how-to books about things they know how to do, counting books, ABC books, books with poems, series books, and on and on. (See Figures 4.10 and 4.11.)

How is the child representing meaning?

Without a doubt, proficient writers are comfortable using written words to hold most of their meaning, but when composing texts, many of them (even those who aren't illustrators) also use other modes of communication—graphics, photos, sketches, audio, video, and the like. This question asks that teachers look at how children are representing meaning in their texts. Is all the meaning in the illustrations, or has the child begun using print symbols as well? If there are print symbols, where is the child in terms of the developmental range of spelling proficiency outlined in Chapter 3? If there is both art and writing, do the two extend each other's meaning in any way? Or are the words simply labeling or narrating the same meanings found in the illustrations?

Over lots of time, the developmental goal is for writers to feel comfortable using written words to hold most of their meanings, though they will likely

① "Deep Blue"

② "Penguins slide on their belly when they get tired."

③ "When penguins lay eggs they keep them on their legs."

④ "They get food from the ocean."

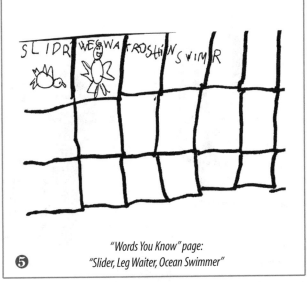

⑤ "Words You Know" page:
"Slider, Leg Waiter, Ocean Swimmer"

FIG. 4.10 *Informational Book About Penguins with a "Words You Know" Box at the End*

❶ How to Make a Gingerbread House: "You get a box."

❷ "You paint it brown."

❸ "You put some of these on."

❹ "You add this on."

❺ "Then you make a sidewalk."

❻ "Then you play with it."

FIG. 4.11 *A How-to Book About Making a Gingerbread House Out of a Cardboard Box*

continue to incorporate other modes of meaning-making as they compose texts throughout their lives.

Understandings About Process

Writing is a process that involves a whole lot of action and decision making from start to finish. Writing *as* a process is not a set of steps writers follow, not by any means, although it is sometimes presented to children as if it were. When they make picture books, children learn to take action and make decisions to get them written. They learn that writing is a process; they can't help but learn this because they cannot make books without going through some kind of process. The main way that writers, proficient and inexperienced alike, learn about the process of moving from an idea to a finished piece of writing is that they live through the process many times.

Teachers, then, need to be watching for and supporting all kinds of developing understandings about writing as a process when young children make books. All the following lines of thinking are meant to help teachers understand this aspect of development.

Is the child intentional about what is being represented on the pages?

Proficient writers understand that when they're writing, everything is under their control, every decision is theirs. It's all about action and decision making. Developing this understanding leads to purposefulness in writing, and for inexperienced writers purposefulness begins with simply being intentional about what they're drawing or writing on the pages.

Growth along this trajectory may move from the child just drawing something in a book and not really intending it to mean anything. When this is the case, often the child's reading of that book will change every time he reads it, and sometimes the child who is drawing with no real intention will ask the teacher what he's drawn. Other children will draw something and decide what it is afterward. This is how the "big giant peanut book" came to be (Figure 4.12). The young writer drew the illustration on the first page, and in the act of drawing, decided it was a big giant peanut. Wisely, once he decided what he had drawn, he followed that idea through the rest of the book.

The developmental goal is, of course, for children to draw and write in their books with a very specific intention guiding them—to *set out* to make some meaning and then move purposefully in that direction. A child who wants to make a book about playing on the playground and draws monkey bars on the

- Is the child intentional about what is being represented on the pages?

- Does the child engage in revision while composing?

- Is there any evidence the child is thinking ahead about what to write?

- Has the child made any intentional crafting decisions?

- How long has the child worked on the book? In one sitting? Over time?

- Does the child exhibit a willingness to solve problems while writing?

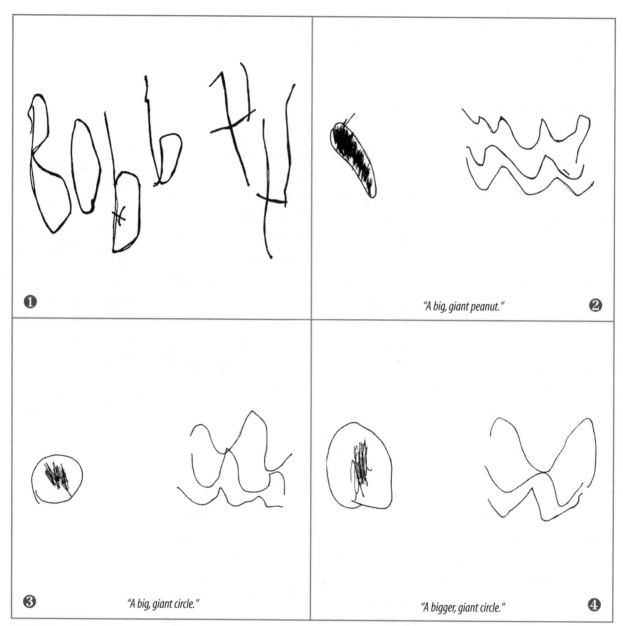

1

2 *"A big, giant peanut."*

3 *"A big, giant circle."*

4 *"A bigger, giant circle."*

FIG. 4.12 *A Big, Giant Peanut Book*

first page, for example, is acting with intention to capture her meaning. Intentionality is a factor in lots of other development too, as you'll see in subsequent lines of thinking.

Does the child engage in revision while composing?

Proficient writers engage in basically five acts of revision: change something, add something, take something out, move something around, or scrap it all and

"The spider has a really long arm and is pulling a rope."

FIG. 4.13   *Revision to Make the Spider's Arm Longer*

start over. Young children can and do act in all these same ways (we've seen them all happen) as they write, mostly revising illustrations; that is, of course, until their written texts become representational. Development in this area ranges from no revision at all (the book is made very quickly and considered finished), to children simply acting to revise something, all the way to the ability to explain why revision decisions are made. After all, proficient writers don't just revise for the sake of revising; they have very specific understandings informing their decisions to make changes.

So much revision happens when children interact with adults around their writing. Allowing them to have markers in their hands when they're telling you about what they've written is really important. The talk seems to help them think about what else they need to do to make their meanings clearer. If you look carefully at Figure 4.13, you can see where the writer extended the spider's arm just as he was explaining to Matt that it had a really long arm and was pulling a rope.

Is there any evidence the child is thinking ahead about what to write?

Proficient writers often think ahead, either loosely or in elaborate detail, about what they will write once they start drafting. Experienced writers continue to think about what will come next once they start drafting. Inexperienced writers tend to start out living very much in the moment of the page they're working on, not thinking ahead at all. With support, however, they learn to think about how a book might go before they even start to represent their meanings on the blank pages, and they continue to think ahead as they draft, as the writer of this *Halloween* book did (Figure 4.14). She explained that the thought bubble on page two was meant to show her thinking about going trick-or-treating with her friends, and before even composing it, she'd planned for the next page to show them out doing just that.

❶ "Me in my Cinderella costume."

❷ "We're going trick-or-treating."
Thought bubble is her thinking about getting candy.

❸ "Yea! My dream came true."

FIG. 4.14 *A child thinks ahead about what she's writing.*

ALREADY READY

Has the child made any intentional crafting decisions?

Proficient writers often do things to make their writing more compelling and engaging, things that go beyond just getting the writing to mean what it's supposed to mean. This repertoire of things writers know how to do to make writing interesting is known as the *craft* of writing (Ray 1999).

Not very many inexperienced writers have a repertoire of crafting techniques at their disposal. They'll have to be shown things other writers do to make their books interesting, things like making the size or color of an illustration match its meaning, or making the last page of a book the same as the first page (a form of repetition). Most of this showing will happen when teachers and children read picture books together.

The writer featured in Figure 4.15 intentionally crafts in an interesting way in his book about a pigeon trapped on top of the school. On pages three and four, he adds talk into the pictures, making his narrative come to life with sound. A technique he's learned from other writers, no doubt, some of them (Mo Willems) who like to write about pigeons too!

Once the craft of writing has become part of what is talked about in the room, teachers can begin watching for and supporting development in this area as children make decisions to intentionally craft their writing.

How long has the child worked on the book?

As we said in Chapter 2, one thing all competent writers have in common is they have developed stamina for the task of writing—both the stamina of one sitting and the stamina to come back and work on the same writing again another day. This question is really meant to help teachers watch and support the development of stamina in writing.

Picture books certainly set children up to have some stamina—it takes a while to put something on all those pages. But you'll still see a real range of development here, from the child who makes a book very quickly and shows no interest in slowing down to even share it with anyone, all the way to the child who comes back to a book for several days. Working alongside another child or two often helps a writer stay with a book a little longer, as does interacting with an adult who is asking questions as the child is writing. The developmental goal really is to have children build their stamina over time in age-appropriate ways. It doesn't really even matter what the child is doing in the book; if she is staying with it, stamina is growing.

Does the child exhibit a willingness to solve problems while writing?

The development of problem-solving behavior in writers is very closely related to the earlier discussion about revision because that is one kind of response a

FIG. 4.15 **A writer uses speech bubbles to craft his writing in an interesting way.**

writer makes when there is a problem. But problem solving actually extends beyond issues revision can resolve, so it's important to consider it as development in its own right. Just as proficient writers do, inexperienced writers will invariably encounter "technical" difficulties along the way—markers don't work, there aren't enough pages in the prestapled book, the book is not finished but it's time to go home, Stephen is sitting in the chair the writer wants to sit in, and on and on. There are so many issues that can keep a writer from writing (just ask proficient writers about this!).

Whenever children are learning to solve problems productively as they make books, this learning should be considered important writing development. The behaviors you might see in this dimension of development will range from simply walking away from writing if problems arise, to figuring out productive solutions to those problems, to just moving forward with writing in spite of them.

Understandings About What It Means to Be a Writer

As children engage in reading and writing over time, they should be developing significant understandings about what it means to be people who write. They should grow to understand themselves in this particular way, and they should be learning what a powerful force writing can be in their lives. All the following questions are designed to help teachers think about a child's growing sense of self as a writer.

- How (and why) has the child decided what to write about?

- How interested is the child in an audience's response?

- Has the child composed in a way that led to new meanings?

- Does the book show that the child willingly took compositional risks?

- Does the child seem to have a sense of self as a writer? A sense of history?

- Does the child show she understands her powerful position as author of the book?

How (and why) has the child decided what to write about?

Part of what helps proficient writers write well is that they choose their topics with care and have good reasons to write about them. One of the real privileges of being a confident writer is the reward of seeing yourself do justice to a topic that matters to you.

Helping children become more intentional about topic selection is important to their overall growth as writers. Developmentally, children demonstrate quite a range of intention as they make topic decisions. Sometimes the topic comes from whatever the child happened to draw on the first page, and sometimes it comes from seeing what another child is writing about. Some children get ideas for books from those shared as read-alouds in the class. Children who have developed more sophisticated understandings about topic selection might decide to write about something because they are interested in it, because it represents their own experience, or because it's a story they've been holding onto in their imagination or from their play.

How interested is the child in an audience's response?

While some writers say they never think of anyone but themselves when they write, many proficient writers compose with a strong sense of audience guiding them, knowing that having an audience represents both a privilege and a responsibility. Proficient writers understand why readers will be motivated to start reading in the first place, and most of them hope to write well enough to keep them reading. Proficient writers usually think a lot about how readers are likely to respond to their writing, and then draft and revise accordingly.

Many inexperienced writers have not yet experienced what it's like for someone to laugh out loud at their writing or to ask them questions about their topics as if they're experts. The more young children experience the response of real readers, the more they will develop the sense of audience that is so essential to proficient writing. Development in this area will range from children showing no interest in sharing their writing with anyone else, to children who are willing to share but seem somewhat disinterested in the response, to children who seek out sharing and truly seem to respond in kind to the responses they receive. The child who asks, "Did you think it was funny?" after someone reads her book, for example, is a child who is developing a sense of audience—a sense that she wants her writing to have the impact on readers she hoped it would have.

The developmental goal is for writers to eventually compose with a sense of audience guiding them, to be thinking about what a reader is going to say or do in response.

Has the child composed in a way that led to new meanings?

For proficient writers, composition is a process that invariably leads them to new understandings about whatever topic they have chosen to address. As a matter of fact, one of the most satisfying things for writers is to be surprised by what their own writing has taught them—the act of writing as much a process of finding meaning as expressing it. We've experienced this surprise time and again as we've written this book.

It may be difficult to imagine that inexperienced writers would develop an understanding of this complex aspect of writing, but some of them do, particularly under the watchful care of adults who know this is an important thing to understand. Remember Jeffrey's book from Chapter 2 about the time his dog Pepper got loose and he had to chase after him. After Jeffrey has Pepper safely back in the garage, the book ends with the joyous declaration, "I love Pepper!" It's just the sort of understanding a writer might come to with new clarity after writing his way through the emotional experience of having lost his beloved dog.

Here are examples of other kinds of comments young writers have made that indicate the act of writing has led them to new meanings.

- ☺ "Hey, I know a lot about tigers."—in response to writing a whole book about tigers

- ☺ "This is kind of a scary book."—before sharing a book that tells the story of being separated from mom in the grocery store

Does the book show that the child willingly took compositional risks?

In the course of writing this book, when people would ask how it was going, we would tell everyone again and again, "Well, it's hard." Sometimes we wondered whether we were even up to the challenge of writing about all we'd learned from working with writers in preschools. But proficient writers have to take risk, to do things that are challenging for them when they write. When the going gets tough, as it inevitably does, even proficient writers just have to try and do it the best they can or they'll never get anywhere.

The good thing about understanding the role of risk-taking in writing development is that inexperienced writers have plenty of opportunities to develop in this dimension. When they first get started, most everything young children want to represent in their writing involves risk and uncertainty about whether they're up to the task or not. Development in this dimension ranges from children saying they don't know how to do something and then avoiding it, to children who say they don't know how to do something but try it anyway, all the way to children who rarely express doubts about their abilities and show great confidence as writers.

Does the child seem to have a sense of self as a writer? A sense of history?

Like anyone else, proficient writers carry many identities around with them. They are gardeners and joggers and motorcycle enthusiasts and knitters. But they are also, of course, writers, and they understand themselves clearly in this particular way. Proficient writers know what kinds of things they write, and why they write them; they know how they write best and which conditions matter; they have plans for writing they'd like to do in the future; and, of course, they have a whole history that's filled with things they've already written. A strong sense of self and history is what keeps writers going even when things get challenging; it is one of the privileges of being a person who writes.

The writing that children are doing—the books they make leaving a tangible record of that writing—should be helping them develop both a sense of self and a sense of history as writers. When a writer like Sean, who you met in Chapter 1, tells people he likes to write about animals because he knows a lot about them, he is forming an understanding of himself as that *particular* sort of writer. When another child learns that two different people have authored and illustrated the book his teacher is getting ready to read and he says, "Oh, I draw all my own pictures," he's showing that he is beginning to see himself as a writer both like and *un*like other writers in the world.

When a child responds to questions about the decisions she's making as she writes, you see further evidence that she is developing a sense of self as a writer. "What made you decide to put a rocket ship in your book?" Matt asked a child once. The book otherwise had nothing at all to do with rocket ships. "That kind of surprised me," he said. Whatever the child said in response wasn't that important because it didn't matter to Matt that there was a rocket ship in the book— lots of unexpected objects show up in books made by four-year-olds. What mattered to Matt was simply that she had a response because a response showed that she was learning to think of herself as a writer who *decides* what will go in her book. This thinking leads us to the last aspect of composition development we'll consider here.

Does the child show she understands her powerful position as author of the book?

You may remember from Chapter 3 how Shayna corrected Matt's reading of her book when he didn't quite get the words right. Her corrections showed that she is developing an important understanding as a writer. She understands that when her name is on it, she *owns* what is in that book and it's up to her to decide everything about it. Proficient writers know that having their names prominently displayed on the front of a book or at the top of an article is, once again, both a privilege *and* a responsibility. Writers own their texts and must *own up* to them, accepting responsibility for all the content and how that content is presented.

Young children have to develop a sense of what true ownership over their writing really means. Because children are so accustomed to adults holding the answers to everything, when they first start writing, some look to adults to tell them what their books are about and what they say. Development in this dimension ranges from the extreme of really no ownership, all the way to the child who confidently corrects all the adults' misconceptions and misreadings of a book and lots of back-and-forth behavior in between.

Perhaps one of the clearest signs that children are developing a sense of their authority as authors is when they confidently answer questions about the writing's content, as opposed to the process. For example, when another child suggests to Shruthi that perhaps the bicycles the princesses are riding in her book should have training wheels on them, Shruthi confidently responds, "Princesses don't need training wheels"; she is clearly and authoritatively owning the content of her writing.

The Privilege and Responsibility of Understanding Composition Development

Just as writers understand that their "membership in the literacy club" (Smith 1988) brings with it both privileges and responsibilities, so too does teachers' membership in the club of "people who understand how much is possible for young writers." We certainly know that the more we've studied and learned about the development of young writers, the more we've had to reevaluate our own membership in this particular teachers' club. As we review the lines of thinking we've laid out here, the significance of them is not lost on us. We feel the privilege of sitting beside children who are writing, but we also feel the tremendous responsibility we have to sit ourselves down next to these writers and do our best to nurture and support them in all the ways they are showing us they're ready to be supported.

Meet Alexis

Author and Illustrator of Circus

Walking into a preschool class one morning, some adults might have been surprised to see four-year-old Alexis sitting at a table engaged in fairly sophisticated research. She had decided to make a book about a circus and had several circus books spread out in front of her. On various pages she had placed sticky notes on pictures that interested her. Clearly, Alexis had a plan for how she wanted to go about making her book and her research had a very "project"-like feel to it. Of course, this sort of purposefulness isn't unusual in this class where children are supported in thinking deeply about what they want to do. On that same morning, another student was working on an ABC book, writing with an equally clear vision of what she was making and how she should go about making it.

Several interesting things happened as Alexis engaged in this research and writing process. In the front of one of the circus books, she found a dedication and asked the teacher about it. Her teacher explained the purpose of a dedication, and Alexis asked whether other books had dedications as well. In response to this question, the two of them set off to find dedications in other books in the classroom. After this ministudy that grew from a question she had as a writer, Alexis decided to dedicate her book to her Mom.

Alexis and her teacher also noticed that the books in her circus research collection were organized into chapters about various aspects of the circus—different types of animals, performers, acts, and so on. As Alexis planned out her book, she easily talked about what would go on each page. She knew she wanted a page with animals and a page that showed a trapeze. She wasn't sure about the last page, but when Alexis got to it, she decided to show what you could find to eat at the circus.

She worked on her book with confidence, and her teacher could see so many ways Alexis was developing as a writer through this process. As the teacher observed Alexis, she decided to build on this confidence and give her a little nudge as a writer. Knowing Alexis had some letter–sound knowledge, her teacher encouraged her to add some writing to each page—to do something a little outside of her comfort zone. To represent important words, Alexis added several letters—writing letters for all the words in her text would have been too overwhelming. Her teacher celebrated this important writing move Alexis had made.

Working from children's positions of strength and capitalizing on their growing confidence, teachers help writers like Alexis outgrow themselves as writers every time they make their way through the process of making books.

❶ *"The circus."*

❷ *"For Mom."*

❸ *"The circus tent was in a storm."*

"There was a monkey, an elephant and a clown."
(Audience is in bottom right corner.) **❹**

❺ *"A girl is on a trapeze."*

"We had a snack. Mr. Glover had popcorn." **❻**

FIG. 4.16 *Alexis' Book, Circus*

The Child's Image of Self as Writer

■ ■

Managing the Balance of Initiation *and* Demonstration

One afternoon, Matt and a group of preschoolers are gathered, talking a little before they read the wonderfully rambunctious book *Silly Sally* by Audrey Wood. The children have read the book before with their teacher, and they're clearly excited about hearing it again. Matt has brought a picture of Wood for the children to see, and he's explaining to them that she is both the author and the illustrator of the book. "She made the words and the pictures," Matt explains. As he says this, Molly speaks up and says, "Hey—just like me!"

Molly's comment that Audrey Wood is "just like me" is telling on so many levels, and knowing about the context in which it was made is critical to understanding its significance. The read-aloud on this day followed some free-choice time, and during that time Molly had worked on a book, *How Molly Became a Pirate*. Melinda Long and David Shannon's book, *How I Became a Pirate* (2003), was no doubt her inspiration. As she and Matt talked, Molly seemed to generate more and more ideas, adding them to the pictures, the print, and her oral storytelling. The book was really quite something by the time she was finished (Figure 5.1).

Just before this time was over, Molly called another child, Alex, over to listen with her as Matt read her book to them in his best read-aloud voice. But rather than looking at Matt as he was reading, Molly watched Alex's face closely as he listened, gauging his responses to the thrilling adventure book she'd written, beaming with delight when he smiled at her story.

Molly's comment that Audrey Wood was just like her happened just a few minutes after this experience, and we believe that one is very much connected to the other. Molly was probably still experiencing a little of the writer's "high" she'd gotten from the response of an audience to her work. This made it so easy for her to see herself in that moment as being like Audrey Wood, another writer

1. "How Molly became a pirate."

2. "This is my house."

3. "This is the pirate ship. They needed me to be a pirate."

4. "Mom is surfing and Dad is relaxing in the sun. Mommy–Daddy, watch out!"

5. "I buried the treasure at my house."

6. "Then I was a pirate again. The end."

FIG. 5.1 **How Molly Became a Pirate**

who makes books that make people smile, just as Molly had made Alex smile with her writing. Of course, we love the confident way Molly put it, stating that Audrey was just like *her*, not that she was like Audrey.

The thing is, children like Molly don't fake a sense of self like this. The genuine, unguarded nature of children's spontaneous comments is so revealing. Molly listened to what Matt was saying about Audrey Wood, and saw something of herself in what she was hearing. Because the adults around her have treated her as the same kind of person as Audrey Wood and Mo Willems and Diane Adams, and because they have made space and time for her to do what these other writers do, Molly is beginning to see herself in this way too. She is developing an image of herself as a writer and sees herself as being like other writers in important ways.

Valuing Children's Image of Themselves as Writers

In the final chapter of this part, "Building Understandings About Young Writers," we'd like to consider how important it is to help children develop an image of themselves as writers—as people who make books. This image is central to all the classroom teaching practices you'll read about in the chapters in Part Two; really, everything we've written about so far has been leading to this critical point of departure. None of the teaching we want to write about makes sense if adults don't first understand how it is that children are just like other people who write (with less experience, of course), and then help them understand this too, as Molly so clearly does.

You may be wondering why a child's image of herself as a writer matters so much. There are two reasons, really. The first is because—at least in Molly's preschool classroom—it matches the adults' image of the children. If adults truly believe preschoolers are capable of engaging in the heady thinking process of composition, then those adults need the children to see themselves as capable too. This shared image helps everyone find a common ground when working together around writing.

The tricky part of this is whether adults *really* see children as capable writers, or whether they just sort of play along with the idea out of politeness. While being polite is certainly a valuable stance to take, it's not the same stance as the respectful one that grows inside adults when they come to see children as truly, remarkably *capable* three- and four-year-old writers. You may remember the discussion in Chapter 1 where we explained that adults must hold two understandings simultaneously: The child is a writer, and the child is four years old. The two don't cancel each other out; they are equally true. As soon as adults get comfortable with this, they begin to see children through new eyes.

The second reason adults value children's image of themselves as writers is because that image is essential to setting composition development in motion. If children don't see themselves as capable of making picture books on their own, they won't have a context in which to engage in the thinking process of writing them on their own. They won't gain valuable experience writing, and experience is the *one thing* young writers need most as new members of the literacy club (Smith 1988). Lack of experience, after all, is what sets them apart from other writers. So it's critical for adults to help children see themselves as capable writers so they will start writing and gain experience.

Writing as an Act of Initiative

While all the lines of thinking in this book have been leading in this direction, we've yet to consider an understanding that has a tremendous impact on children's image of themselves as writers. The understanding has to do with who *initiates* the act of writing—who sets it in motion by deciding, "I am going to make a book (or a sign or a list or a letter or . . .)." Respecting that act of initiative is a stance adults must take if children are to see themselves as writers.

Think for a moment about what it really means for a child (or any person for that matter) to decide she is going to make a book as Molly did on this morning. Her act of initiative is driven by two dispositions: desire and belief. Molly wants to write a book and believes she is capable of doing it. In terms of Molly seeing herself as a writer, desire and belief are clearly codependent dispositions. If she doesn't believe she is capable of making a book, then she's not likely to initiate writing one on her own. If Molly doesn't write books on her own, she's not likely to think of herself as being just like Audrey Wood. She must believe that she is capable of doing what Wood does in her very own, four-year-old way.

Someone who initiates an act of writing, and particularly a person who initiates an act of writing like making a book, possesses both the desire to write and the belief that he or she is capable of writing. What's important for teachers to understand is how critical it is to support both dispositions—desire and belief— because they form the very core of the child's image of himself or herself as a capable writer. Let's consider those two dispositions now—first, desire.

Supporting Desire: Helping Children Want to Make Books

Throughout *Already Ready*, we've said more than once that preschool children choose whether they will make books or not, but that making books is clearly an activity that is privileged and encouraged by teachers. That students choose to make books, rather than being told they *must* make them, matters for several reasons. As it relates to this discussion, however, choice matters because *initiative* matters. Building a sense of agency (Johnston 2004) and initiative in children who are just beginning to write is foundational to all the learning they will do throughout their lives as writers.

For the most part, simply putting a writing center in place is *not* enough to build children's sense of initiative for writing. You can't just "build it and they will come," in other words. In a classroom filled with all sorts of interesting possibilities from which they may choose, how do teachers help children believe they really want to write and build that desire in them? We'd like to suggest three main ways privileging and encouraging the making of books happens: 1) creating energy around read-alouds, 2) inviting individual children to make books, and 3) sharing children's books with others.

Creating Energy Around Read-Alouds

From the very start, as teachers read professionally published picture books aloud to children, they begin suggesting:

> You know, you could make a picture book like this if you'd like. We
> have everything you need here to make one of these if you want.
> You could put in pictures and words, just like Eric Carle does. And
> you could even make your book be about anything you want . . .

They show children the prestapled books and markers and generally just "talk-up" book-making as if it is something that children, of course, will want to do. Connecting this first encouragement to picture books by professional authors is important because those books help children have a vision for what a book would be if they were to try to make one.

Beyond encouraging children to want to make picture books, in Chapter 7 we'll explain how read-alouds are also such an important teaching context for helping children learn many things that will nudge their composition development once they start making books.

Inviting Individual Children to Make Books

The power of suggestion is, well, powerful. After all, it's one thing to talk about how someone—anyone—might make a book; it's quite another to talk with Shane and suggest, "You know, Shane, *you* could make a book about that." Teachers are on the lookout for opportunities to invite individual children to make books. Sometimes children have no interest in the teacher's invitation, but sometimes they do. The little bits of encouragement seem to be the leg up some preschoolers need to move in that direction. The following list contains some common scenarios where teachers might invite children to make books.

- If a child is excited to tell a story about something that happened outside of school, then after the story is shared orally, suggest she make a book about it.

- After children act out a story in their dramatic play, suggest they make that story into a book while it's still fresh in their minds.

- When classroom activities create energy and a "buzz" of talk around them, suggest that children make books about what has happened.

- When it's clear that a child knows a lot about something, suggest that he make a book to teach other people about the topic.

- After making or building something, suggest making a book to teach others how to do what was just done.

- If you know a perfect audience and occasion for a child's writing, say a grandmother coming to visit or a big brother's birthday, suggest the child make a book for that person or occasion.

- If you haven't seen a child make a book (in a while—or ever), you might simply suggest, "You know, I'd love to see you make a book. I haven't watched you write in a while (before)."

In addition to specific invitations, suggestive hints as teachers interact with children can nudge them toward book-making. Saying things like, "If you decide to make a book today, be sure to let me know." Or "If you make a book today, what's it going to be about?" These kinds of statements can plant the idea for writing in a child's thinking.

After working with children who are making books, Matt likes to ask, "What's your next book going to be about?"—a kind of question he calls "positive presupposition." Remember that the point is not for teachers to be pushy; the point is to be suggestive and encouraging. Initiative will come as the possibilities for writing look more and more promising to children. The teacher's role is to help them imagine the possibilities. A big part of this imagining is actually teaching children about where people get ideas for writing, and indeed, why anyone would take the initiative to write in the first place.

Sharing Children's Books with Others

When children do take the initiative to make books, it's important that those books be shared with others in ways that privilege and encourage *more* book-making. The talk and energy around the sharing of books is contagious, so filling a classroom with book-sharing does important teaching work for several reasons.

First, just as it is for all writers, finding interested readers for children's books is one of the best insurances that they'll choose to make books again in the future. Response from readers is motivating for many writers, and three- and four-year-olds are generally no different. Now, having said that, when they make their *first* books, children may not understand that reading and sharing with others is going to be part of the deal. They're not expecting readers that first time out, in other words. But as they experience the responses of readers more and more, they'll begin to expect responses and write with that in mind.

Another reason sharing books is important is because seeing them helps other children believe they can make books too. Once children see that a book made by a four-year-old *looks* like it was made by a four year old, they understand exactly what the teacher means by suggesting they make books. If the only vision they have of picture books comes from professionally published ones, some children may have trouble believing they can actually make them on their own.

Related to this when children's books are shared with other children, thoughtful teachers can point out all sorts things about how they were made that provide important demonstrations of the thinking process of writing. In Chapter 10, we'll explain the kinds of things teachers help children notice about other children's books that can do important teaching work.

Sharing the books children have made with others doesn't need to be fancy. It can be as simple as calling another child or several children over to listen to a child's book, or other adults in the room or in the school might be solicited to be interested audiences. Also, a regular routine of having children gather for a "share time" around their book-making privileges and encourages the making of books in significant ways.

Remember, when books children have made are not yet representational, teachers have to be sure to share those books with readers in thoughtful ways. Either the children who wrote them must be present to read their books, or an adult who has heard a child's book several times and knows how it goes can share it with others. If a teacher is sharing a child's book with others, it's a good idea to have the child standing there as it is shared. Actually, the teacher's read-aloud voice often does the child's writing more justice than the writer's read-aloud voice can, particularly if he is shy.

Supporting Belief: Respecting Children's Initiative

When a child decides, "I think I would like to make a book," it's irrelevant whether the decision was made because of a teacher's suggestion or whether the child decided to make a book on his own. The decision to actually do it—to sit down and make a book—is the initiative teachers are hoping for, and everything about how they respond to that child's decision matters. Remember that wanting to make a book and believing you are capable of making one are two different dispositions. Some children will want very much to make a book, but won't believe they can make one without someone there to help them. Helping children believe they are capable writers who can make their own books begins by respecting their initiative.

What does it mean to respect a child's initiative? First and foremost, we believe it means that we must respect the child for the writer he or she is at this moment in time. If three-year-old Charlie comes over, takes some prestapled paper and markers, and begins making a book, we can't ask him *not to be three* as he's doing it. We can't expect that his writing will look like ours, or even that it will look like someone's writing much closer to Charlie's age. As a matter of fact, we can't have any preconceived notions about what his writing should look like until we see what he does (Figure 5.2). In other words, we can't ask Charlie to be a writer and not be Charlie!

We believe the most important thing a teacher can do to support a child's belief in himself as a writer is to send the clear and unequivocal message that he is valued as the writer he is at this moment in time, and that whatever this child can do is okay. That's all teachers should be asking of children, "Come to this table and be the writer you are at this moment in time." And if they come, as Charlie did on this morning, teachers need to be waiting for them, ready to welcome them into the club of people who write. Matt rolled out the welcome mat as he listened to Charlie talk intently about his writing, even though a variety of language issues made it very difficult for Matt to understand what he was saying. But because of Matt's teaching actions, Charlie left the table that morning convinced that he could make a book and talk about it with someone who was interested. More important, because of Matt's teaching actions, Charlie will no doubt *come back* to the table again.

Keeping the message that children are valued for the writers they are clear and unequivocal helps them believe they are capable, but it does so much more than this. When children see themselves as capable writers, they sit down and show us what they are able to do, and this is how we know what to teach them. This is, perhaps, the ultimate show of respect for the initiative the child has taken to come to the table as a writer. The teacher's words and actions send the message: "Show me what you can do, and then I'll help you get a little better at it."

On the morning that three-year-old Charlie made his book, he showed Matt that he was ready to learn about how what he puts on paper should mean something. Matt had observed him using the markers sort of haphazardly and suspected Charlie might not yet be drawing with meaningful intention. In a

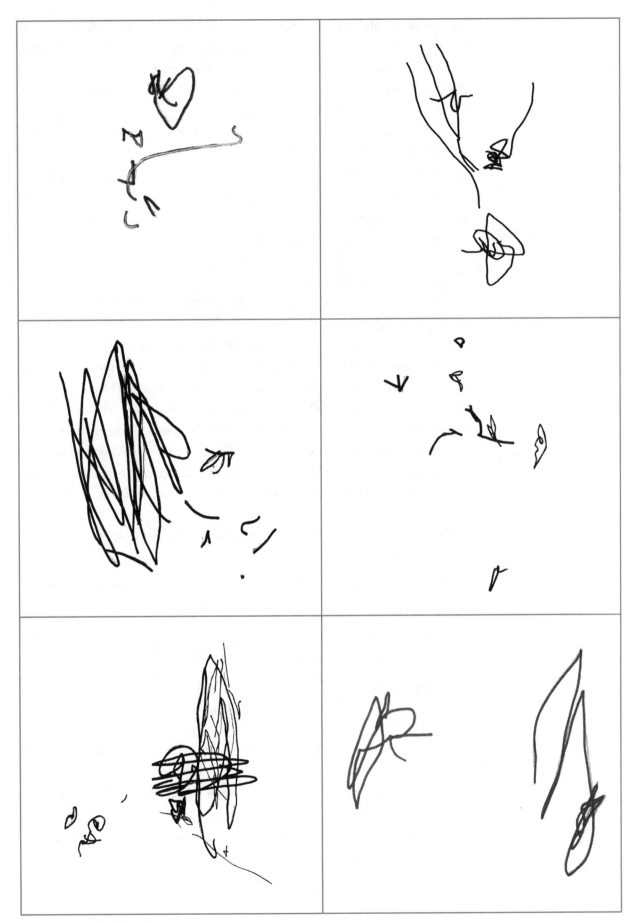

FIG. 5.2 *Charlie's Book*

thoughtful teaching move, Matt pulled out his favorite line to use when he's not really sure what the child has drawn and for whatever reason he isn't helping him understand. Matt said, "Wow. Look at that. You've made purple lines on the paper and they go in all different directions." This comment is what led Charlie to begin talking about his book.

Because Matt simply named what he saw on the paper and what it represented to him, he helped Charlie begin to understand this very important aspect of writing. What a writer puts on the page should mean something, both to the writer and to other people. It might take quite a while for Charlie to understand this with lots of depth, but to Matt, it seemed to be a good nudging point based on where Charlie was as a writer at that time.

The Influence of Vygotsky

"Show me what you can do, and then I'll help you get a little better at it." If this sounds very Vygotskian, that's because it is. Like so many before us, our thinking about teaching and learning has been shaped profoundly by the work of Lev Vygotsky, and particularly the theoretical construct known as the zone of proximal development (ZPD). When a child sits down to write and shows a teacher what he is able to do and what he seems to understand about what he is doing, he is showing that teacher what Vygotsky (1978) would call his actual developmental level: "functions that have already matured, that is, the end products of development" (86). Charlie showed Matt that he seemed to understand and could do several things when it came to making a book, including that:

- a marker is used to make symbols on paper: He was able to use markers in that way.

- print and illustrations in a book stretch across the pages: He was able to stay with it and put something on each page.

- writers use the blank space on the page in different ways: He positioned his markings in a variety of places on the paper.

- print and drawing are different: Some of his markings do appear more linear and hint at this understanding, which is truly emergent.

Vygotsky would argue that what Charlie can do on his own, his actual development, doesn't give us the full picture of his capabilities because "with assistance, every child can do more than he can by himself" (1986, 187). If his teachers are to respect his act of initiative, they must help Charlie truly realize how capable he is as a writer, and this means helping him see not only what he can do, but also what he can do with some assistance.

This is why we say Charlie "seems" to understand these things about making a book. It could be that he is actually watching what the other children are doing around him and following along. Vygotsky says that "children can imitate a variety of actions that go well beyond the limits of their own capabilities. Using imitation, children are capable of doing much more in collective activity or under the guidance of adults" (1978, 88). Charlie may simply be acting *as if* he understands and is able, but at some point there will no longer be a difference between "acting as if" and simply acting. When this happens his development will have moved forward.

Understanding what kind of assistance to give children is at the very heart of understanding the ZPD. The zone represents the distance between what the child can do independently—imagine Charlie at a table making a book by himself—and the potential level of his development that can be reached with some assistance. Now, imagine him again at that table with other children and a teacher. The key word is *proximal*, which means, of course, "situated close to." Vygotsky (1986) explains the importance of proximity in assisting development:

> With assistance, every child can do more than he can by himself—though only within the limits set by the state of his development. If imitative ability had no limits, any child would be able to solve any problem with an adult's assistance. But this is not the case. The child is most successful in solving problems that are closer to those solved independently; then the difficulties grow until, at a certain level of complexity, the child fails, whatever assistance is provided. (187)

The teaching we do as young children are writing, then, must be designed to help them do and understand just a little more than they are able to do and to understand on their own. To accomplish this, teachers need not only a clear picture of where the child is now in his development but also a sense of where he might go next. To quote Vygotsky (1978) one more time: "The only 'good learning' is that which is in advance of development" (89). But remember, not too far in advance; the assistance needs to be *proximal*.

When Matt decided to assist Charlie by engaging him in talking about what his drawings might mean, he was supporting this young writer's composition development in a very important way. Matt was helping Charlie understand that when he's composing, what he puts on paper should mean something. By expanding the framework of writing development to include understandings about composition, teachers can work so much more intentionally within children's different zones of proximal development. After all, if the only writing development a teacher can envision for a child is connected to transcription (spelling and handwriting), that teacher is very limited in the assistance he or she might offer a writer like Charlie. At this point in his development as a writer, transcription is so far outside Charlie's zone of proximal development that there is really no way to give him "just a little assistance" with it. With this understanding, we turn an important corner and must next consider a very common practice in the teaching of young children: dictation.

Problematizing the Practice of Dictation

Although the chapters explaining teaching practices that support young writers are yet to come, no doubt you already suspect you won't be reading in them about how to take dictation from children who initiate writing on their own. In its most common form, dictation as a teaching practice involves a child drawing (and sometimes writing) what he can on his own, and then an adult writes the words the child wants on the paper or in the book. We want to be very clear here about our reasons for believing dictation is not the best practice to support a young writer who has initiated writing on his or her own.

First, you may remember that much earlier in this chapter we discussed how important it is for teachers to consider "who *initiates* the act of writing—who sets it in motion by deciding, 'I am going to make a book' (or a sign or a list or a letter or . . .)." If someone three or four decides she wants to write, does what she can, and then takes it to an adult who writes her words for her, the message of that action is clear and unequivocal: Adults, not children, are the ones who really know how to write. This, of course, is the exact opposite clear and unequivocal message we want to send: "You're a writer and you're four and you're writing just like someone who is four should be writing and we think that's amazing."

The practice is so off-message, in fact, that it complicates all sorts of interactions adults might have with children that could help them grow as writers. As explained earlier, if children don't show us what they understand and know how to do, we don't know what makes sense to teach them. In classrooms where dictation is a common practice, adults often fail to see the onset of actual transcription development because the children aren't trying very hard to get the words down. They know they don't have to try. And the adults aren't really looking for transcription development either because, as long as they're taking dictation, they're not thinking about how they might be helping children figure out how to get the words down on their own, if they're ready.

Interestingly enough, once children do show us they are beginning to understand how letters and sounds work together to make words, dictation as a form of assistance is way outside the ZPD because an accurately transcribed message is still a very long way off in terms of what is possible for them. We believe helping children develop new strategies for spelling and understandings about how the spelling system works is a much better way to nudge their development forward. As a matter of fact, by the time an accurately transcribed text (rendered through dictation) is *proximal* to a child's actual development, there will be no need for it. When the ZPD is used as a rationale for dictation, the rationalization is flawed because adults aren't *helping* children do something they're not quite doing on their own; adults are doing it for them, and helping and doing are very different endeavors.

Knowing what a common and well-meaning practice dictation is in early childhood settings, for several years now we've been carefully weighing all the reasons we can find for why adults believe it makes sense as a teaching practice with young writers. For each of them, we seem to be left with a "yes, but" conundrum, and in our thinking, none of the *yes*'s seem to make the *but*'s worth the practice. Let's consider a few of these next.

Honoring Words

Taking dictation shows children that adults honor their words and find them important enough to record. Yes, but adults can honor children's words in so many other ways that don't come at the cost of the message of dictation. As adults work alongside young writers, they honor their words by saying them back in their best read-aloud voices and remembering them and sharing them with anyone who will listen. Adults honor children's words when they ask questions about them, and when they laugh and sigh and gasp in response to those words.

Helping with a Difficult Task

Taking dictation keeps children from getting overly fatigued and frustrated by trying to write themselves. Yes, but if children are getting overly fatigued and frustrated, it's because what they are being asked to do—or what they *believe* they are being asked to do—is too difficult for them. The task is outside their zone of proximal development. Children who are painting don't get frustrated with painting; they get frustrated only when they have an image that their painting should be something that it's not. If teachers respect children's initiative to write and accept them as the writers they are, then children should not be frustrated by their efforts. If they are frustrated, then something is amiss; dictation will only bandage it, not solve the problem in any long-term, productive way.

Knowing It Isn't Right

Some children know what writing looks like and are frustrated because their writing doesn't look like other writing. Taking dictation relieves this frustration. Yes, but we believe children are better served by understanding why "other" writing looks the way it does and why their writing looks the way it does—because they are three and four and just learning how it all goes. And it's likely that the only way they'll get better at how it all goes, of course, is to keep writing. Couple this understanding with showing children how much smarter and more resourceful (than adults) they have to be as they're writing, and celebrate their smart resourcefulness often.

Capturing Rich Writing

Taking dictation helps capture the richness of children's oral language and storytelling in a way their own writing can't possibly capture. Yes, and children's oral language development will outpace their writing development—especially in terms of the stamina and fluency to capture it all—for a long time. As writers, children must be helped to become comfortable with this fact or they will be frustrated by their own efforts. But instead of dictation, adults can simply encourage children to say all those rich words and tell all those rich stories—over and over—in conjunction with whatever words and illustrations they're able to get on paper. It's fine, in other words, for the talk to be bigger than the writing.

There's another *but* to this one too. When adults want to capture the richness of children's oral language and storytelling by taking dictation, we have to ask, "Capture it for whom?" Oral language development also greatly outpaces children's reading development for a long time, so most aren't able to read back the words they've dictated. Only proficient readers have access to those words. If adults need a record of children's language to help *them* capture and remember it, then they should record it somehow, either in personal written notes or on an audio recorder.

Making Sense of Their Writing

Taking dictation helps parents make sense of children's writing. Yes, but a dictated text is not *necessary* for parents to make sense of children's writing. As long as the child is present he or she can share the writing in the same way it's shared at school. As children share their writing on their own terms, they can help their parents not only understand what they're writing but also, more important, help them understand their writing *development*. Of course, parents don't always understand this, so at Matt's school, a regular newsletter does the important work of helping parents understand the types of literacy development they should be looking for and supporting in interactions with their children. (Appendix A shows an example of a parent newsletter.) Sharing some information about students' writing with parents, which certainly may include notes on what the writing says, can sometimes help parents really appreciate their children's true writing development.

Helping Them Know How to Write

Taking dictation shows children how writing goes down on the page—how their spoken words become written words (letter formation, spelling, word spacing, directionality, punctuation, etc.). Yes, dictation can serve all these purposes, and children should have opportunities to see how experienced writers take spoken words and turn them into written words. *But,* there are two critical issues to consider here.

First, as a teaching demonstration, what dictation shows children about writing—how someone accurately transcribes—is so far outside the ZPD for most preschoolers that it's highly questionable whether dictation is very meaningful for writers at this point in their development. For very young writers, the value of watching an adult write down the words they've said is probably more in how it simply demystifies the physical way marks get on paper.

The demonstration of transcription provided by dictation better serves children who are further along in their development, those who have begun to experiment with the letter–sound system and are developing some understandings about how that system works. And even for these children, the practice is probably much more valuable when they are involved in the process as they are in closely aligned practices, such as shared and interactive writing. If children are at this point in their development, which can only be discerned if they are writing for themselves, then adults need to find opportunities to demonstrate often how spoken words become written words and all that's involved in that process.

This leads to the second critical issue worth considering. We believe using dictation to demonstrate writing should happen in contexts *where children have not initiated writing on their own.* If children decide they want to write, we believe their acts of initiative should be respected, as we've explained throughout this chapter. But every day in preschool classrooms, opportunities *abound* for teachers to initiate writing in collaboration with children, and when teachers initiate the writing, they create a meaningful context to show children how their spoken words become written words.

Consider the following scenarios during which a teacher might take children's words and write them as a demonstration:

- Writing down observations about something the class has studied together

- Writing ideas for something the class is brainstorming

- Inviting children to coauthor a book the teacher wants to write

- Recording class news and announcements

- Writing an account of something the class has experienced together— for example, taking a walk outside

- Making a list of things needed to complete a project

Whatever the context that gives rise to it, when the teacher is the one who takes the initiative and decides to write, the message of this action is not that the teacher is writing because the children cannot. The message is that the teacher is writing because it was his or her idea to write in the first place. And the demonstration that dictation provides—whatever that might be for children at different places in their development—is there without paying the high price of the wrong message.

What we are suggesting then, is that the question of whether dictation is a valuable practice or not requires a more complex response than "yes" or "no." A thoughtful response requires us to engage in "both/and" thinking, as explained in the NAEYC's position statement on developmentally appropriate practice (1997, 15). As this statement makes clear, so many practices cannot be understood in simple either/or terms—either a practice is developmentally appropriate or it is not—and dictation is one of those practices. We hope our discussion of it here has made clear our *both/and* position with regard to dictation, a position that takes context and message into account as it considers the value of the practice.

Our teaching practices do matter, not only for the content they provide but also for the messages they send children about who we believe them to be. As Douglas Barnes (1992) said: "We cannot make a clear distinction between the content and the form of the curriculum, or treat the subject matter as the end and the communication as no more than a means. The two are inseparable" (15). Our hope is that the consistent message of the teaching practices you will read about in the following chapters is that children are capable writers—or as Molly would say, they're writers just like Audrey Wood—and their teachers are privileged to be teaching and learning alongside them.

Meet Nick

Author and Illustrator of Trixie

Mo Willems' books, including *Don't Let the Pigeon Drive the Bus* and *Knuffle Bunny*, are favorites in many of the preschool classes in Matt's school, so it's not surprising that three-year-old Nick became particularly interested in these books.

Nick and his classmates read them so often with their teacher, they began to think of Mo as their friend, and they talked about him as if they knew him. Nick became particularly interested in the decisions Mo made as the author and illustrator of *Knuffle Bunny*. He wanted to know why Mo has several of the characters walking out of the pictures. He wondered why Mo made Trixie look like she has six arms when she's excitedly trying to get her dad's attention. He asked why Mo made the picture break apart like a "storm" when the dad finally understands what Trixie is trying to tell him. Nick noticed details big and small throughout the book, and he eagerly pointed out his discoveries to his friends and any adult who happened to pop into the class.

Naturally, Nick started making books that incorporated some of the features he admired in Mo Willems' books. Notice Knuffle Bunny's arms on the page from one of Nick's books.

As a way of supporting their understanding that Willems is a real person and an author, Nick's teacher showed him and his classmates Mo's website where they learned more about him. Nick discovered that there was a place where he could email Mo. Nick sent a message packed with questions, including asking Mo whether he'd ever written a book where Trixie was big and the daddy was little. Willems replied and said this sounded like a great idea, and he suggested Nick write a book like that. Of course, a suggestion like this from his new friend, Mo Willems, resulted in Nick beginning work on a book right away.

Here's the book Nick sent to Mo. Notice how Trixie is actually very big on the first page and on the next page the daddy is actually smaller. The storm on the last page is related to the lightning-type way the photo breaks apart in *Knuffle Bunny*.

The somewhat disconnected narrative of this book may seem incongruent with his complex thinking about it, but remember, Nick was only three when he wrote *Trixie*. Only three, and yet because he saw himself as being like Mo Willems in important ways, Nick was able to learn from his favorite author, just as so many experienced writers learn from their chosen mentors.

After emailing Mo and being inspired to write *Trixie*, Nick learned that Mo already had plans to write another *Knuffle Bunny* book that takes place when Trixie is older. Nick is fairly sure he's the one who gave this idea to Mo!

"It's Trixie and her mouth is big.
That's her name on her shirt. She has curly hair."

FIG. 5.3   *Nick's Book*

"A little head, little legs, little eyes, little mouth, and little arms.
The hands are going up and down.
That's the daddy when he is little."

❶

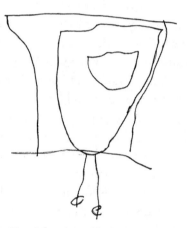

"Now the mommy is playing with blocks.
It's a big block. And a bad, mad mouth."

❷

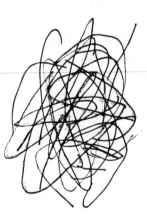

❸   "This is the storm. Her have an umbrella. Her hold the baby."

FIG. 5.4   *Nick's Book, Trixie*

PART TWO

Teaching Practices That Nurture Young Writers

Understanding the Teaching Context

In Part One, we explained some essential understandings about young writers and the conditions that support them. We attempted to build a case for a few key ideas:

- Young children are like any other writers, just with less experience.

- Functional writing and compositional writing require different stances, and people with strong writing identities are comfortable with both.

- Children who make picture books are engaging in complex thinking about writing as a process.

- Using writing to compose involves much more than transcription.

- Composition development is multidimensional.

- Supporting a child's image of self as a writer is critical to his or her overall development.

With these ideas informing them, Chapters 7 through 10 in Part Two explore the nature of teaching practices that support young writers and help them thrive. Before moving on to specific practices, however, this chapter revisits some important ideas about the preschool classrooms in which these practices are situated, and couches them in the context of the NAEYC guidelines for developmentally appropriate practice.

Preschool Classrooms That Nurture Young Writers

The Importance of Choice

Because the focus of this book is on writing, it may seem like all children ever do in these classrooms is make books, but that's not the case of course. Preschool children are allowed to choose when and if they will make books, and they choose book-making from a variety of other engagements, including playing, making things, exploring, reading, baking, painting, building, acting, observing, singing, and so on. Engagements that involve *thriving*, if you will. Preschoolers thrive in active, hands-on environments, and books are just one of many things they may—or may not—get their hands on in the course of a day.

Choosing to make books matters, as we explained in Chapter 5, because initiative matters, especially if very young children are to craft an image of themselves as writers. If they're simply rotating through predetermined center activities, then children are making books because they are scheduled to make them, not because they've thought of something they'd like to make a book about and taken the initiative to make it. Choosing to write comes from a very different place and sense of self in young children than writing because it's what they've been told to do.

Many children will eventually move into writing workshops in kindergarten or in later grades, and in these workshops, they will write because they've been told it's time to, not because they've chosen to write. This is because writing development in later grades will become much more of a focus in the curriculum. But in preschool, writing is all about awareness and exploration (NAEYC and IRA 2005), as are so many other areas of development. We believe setting up conditions where children choose to write is the best way to support this.

On Writing and Play

In addition to making books, children in preschool classrooms are also encouraged to use writing as part of their play and exploration. The functional writing children do in support of other activities helps them understand the many ways writing can be used as a tool to get things done in the world. Paper and markers of all kinds are strategically placed around the room, and adults often encourage children to use writing in functional ways—making signs and notes and lists and the like—as they observe and interact with them in different engagements. Figure 6.1 shows a letter Ella wrote and sent to Matt, thanking him for loaning her his Leonardo book and asking that he come meet with her to talk about it.

Ella's thank-you letter to Matt.

FIG. 6.1 ***Ella's Letter to Matt***

We should also mention that sometimes children take writing and art supplies and simply play with them, exploring the potential of the various tools, seemingly much more interested in the process than in the products they are creating (Rowe 1994). But when children choose to make books, an interesting shift happens.

Instead of writing *as part* of other play and exploration, writing *becomes* the play and exploration in which children engage. In fact, the energy of children making books should look and sound and feel like the energy they bring to other dramatic play. Children should play "writer" and make books with the same verve that they play "baker" and bake cakes or play "pilot" and fly the plane.

We need to be very clear here however. Encouraging them to make books in the same way they engage in other play in no way means that children's efforts as writers are devalued or not to be taken seriously. Adults recognize that there is really no distinction—in terms of thinking and action—between children who believe they are playing at writing and writing itself. Playfulness is simply an attitude adults want children to bring to their writing, a spirit and a stance, a belief that anything is possible. As the NAEYC (1997) position statement on developmentally appropriate practice makes so clear: "Play is an important vehicle for children's social, emotional and cognitive development, as well as a reflection of their development" (8). Teachers of the youngest writers totally embrace a playful stance to writing because they realize how critical this stance is to nurturing children's development on so many levels.

The NAEYC position statement goes on to say that "child-initiated, teacher-supported play is an essential component in developmentally appropriate practice" (1997, 9). In many ways, these two adjectives capture what's essential about writing and making books in preschool classrooms: It's child-initiated and teacher-supported. The child-initiated part reminds us of the importance of choice, and the teacher-supported part reminds us that children should not be left alone to play at writing—they need support. Teacher support is, in fact, the focus of the entire second half of this book.

The Social Nature of Book-Making

Another key feature of the preschool classrooms where these writing practices are situated is the social nature of making books. Occasionally, there is only one child who's chosen to make a book at a given time, but in fact this rarely happens. In the natural following-along that young children are apt to do, seeing one writer busy making something invariably makes other writers want to join in. And sometimes the joining in is not motivated so much by a desire to make a book as it is a gesture of friendship. "I want to do what my friend is doing" is the motivation, and if your friend is making a book, you make one too. Simply having multiple chairs at the table with all the writing supplies available encourages children to join others as they're writing.

When several children are making books at the same time, they learn so much from interacting and watching each other. Matt watched Blake once for several minutes as he drew all sorts of marks on his paper, but all Matt's attempts to get Blake to tell him what he was drawing were fruitless. Blake just kept busy—and silent—while Matt had a one-sided conversation with him. After several minutes, AJ joined the table, sat down with a book and markers, and immediately began talking. "I'm making a truck," he announced. Matt restated what he said, "AJ is making a truck." Then, without missing a beat, Blake finally spoke up and said, "I'm putting my mom." Matt's questions had been unsuccessful in helping Blake bring meaning to his drawing, but the demonstration of another four-year-old was just what he needed to help him understand he was supposed to draw something meaningful on the page.

Encouraging social interactions with peers as children are writing is critical. As the NAEYC position statement makes clear: "Children are active learners, drawing on direct physical and social experience as well as culturally transmitted knowledge to construct their own understandings of the world around them" (1997, 7). When Blake heard the way AJ talked about his writing, quite likely it represented a new way of talking about writing for him. The social experience caused Blake to rework his understanding of his role in this sort of conversation, to form a new *register* as Halliday (1975) called it—a new understanding for a kind of talk that's connected to a particular situation. In a situation like this, the impact of peer demonstration is often profound because children see themselves as being so much more *like* their peers than like the adults around them. Blake could imagine himself talking about writing better when he heard someone a lot more like him—another four-year-old writer—talk in this way.

Because making books and sharing books with others is such a valued literacy engagement in these preschool classrooms, there is quite a bit of social motivation for children to make them. In other words, it's difficult to resist because "everybody's doing it." Book-making gets talked about, talked up, and talked around most any time a child chooses to engage in it, and this message—that book-making is privileged in the society of the classroom—is clear.

In her study of a preschool classroom, Rowe (1994) also found that social motivation was a significant factor in children choosing to engage in literacy activities—activities she calls the "coin of the realm" because of the high value placed on them. She explains it in this way:

> Teachers always responded positively to children's attempts to express themselves in writing or art, and peers responded positively more often than not. In order to participate fully in the life of this classroom, both teachers and children necessarily became authors of their own texts and audiences for other members of the community . . . [and] the most compelling and immediate reason to explore print or art was to gain access to classroom interaction. (191)

Teachers Are Writers Too

Children in preschool classrooms see their teachers writing in all the same ways they are encouraged to write, and the demonstrations of these more experienced members of the literacy club are important as well. As Frank Smith (1988) says, children want to join the club, before they even know much about reading and writing, "because they can see others engaging profitably in literacy activities who are the kind of people the children see themselves as being" (10). The "others" children see engaging profitably in literacy activities will certainly be their peers, as discussed earlier, but seeing *others* with more experience is key because experienced readers and writers can be resources for children in ways peers cannot be. Children need more experienced writers to be their "unwitting collaborators" (Smith 1988, 10) when they're just starting out, and they need access to what experienced writers know and understand.

Teachers of preschool children, then, are mindful of what their actions demonstrate about writing. It's not enough for them just to see teachers writing; children need to see teachers writing and also to understand that writing is a *profitable* endeavor. The difference is subtle, but important. For example, children might see their teacher making notes as she moves about the class and interacts with them during the morning. By itself, this is certainly an important demonstration. But its significance grows when the teacher later shares something from her notes, reading from them and commenting on them in ways that let children see how important it was for her to write things down in the first place. The key is to keep in mind that when children see teachers using writing for functional purposes—making lists, jotting notes, writing reminders, posting signs—they also need to see this writing serve its intended purpose.

In a preschool classroom where making books is privileged and encouraged, children need to see that their teachers find this kind of writing to be profitable as well. Sometimes teachers make books on their own and then share these already-written books with children. Matt writes a lot about his family in his books, and he often shares them with children in conjunction with read-alouds or during share times.

When he shares his own books, Matt is careful to talk about how and why he chose his topic and about the different decisions he made along the way as he was writing. For instance, he might explain why he decided to zoom in on his daughter's face in an illustration to show she was angry, or why he used a repeating line throughout his book to connect his ideas. When he shares both his writing and his *thinking about writing*, he provides children with a demonstration they can't get from the authors of professionally published picture books because the authors and illustrators of them are not present. As we explained in Chapter 5, when Matt shares his thinking about writing, he is providing a demonstration that is much closer to the zone of proximal development for most preschoolers than a demonstration of accurate transcription would be.

Sometimes teachers make books as they're sitting beside children, and they talk about what they're thinking and doing as they make them. This kind of talk makes an experienced writer's process public and available as a demonstration for children. In this particular interaction, they learn about the process of writing, drawing, and composing, but children also learn how it is that a writer talks about process and decision making—a kind of talk teachers invite children to do as they write.

Making *Books*: An Intentional Verb Choice

A single word can make so much difference, and in preschool classrooms where children make books, the verb *make* is just that kind of word. The word has been thoughtfully settled on as the best word—both in meaning and in connotation—to name the action children are invited to take when they compose their own picture books. Although it may seem odd to include this particular verb choice in a discussion of key features of classrooms that support young writers, we believe the common use of *making* in the social language of preschool classrooms is quite significant.

First, the word *make* is a good project word because it implies both intention and fashioning. "I am going to *make* a book" suggests a person is going to do some things on purpose to fashion something in a particular way. The lunge toward understanding writing as composition, as bringing many elements together into a unified whole, is implicit in the fashioning sense of the word *make*. "Making" doesn't just happen by accident; someone has to set out to make something, and helping children act with intention to fashion something as writers is very important to their ongoing development.

Make is also a much more open-ended invitation to meaning-making than either *draw* or *write*—the main actions children take when they make books. *Make* suggests a range of actions in a way the other verbs do not. Before children have had a chance to develop an image of themselves as writers and illustrators, the range of actions suggested by *make* helps more of them see themselves as capable. A child who thinks he's not yet ready to *write* a book may see himself as perfectly capable of *making* one. And teachers, of course, want children to explore a range of options for making meaning when they compose, so having a word that suggests this serves this purpose as well.

An Expanded Definition of Reading

The final key idea about preschool classrooms should already be clear: Where preschoolers are strongly supported in their writing development, teachers have embraced a multimodal, expanded definition of writing to include any and all efforts to *represent* meaning on the page. Drawing and writing are viewed as collaborative processes and are equally valued when children are making their books because teachers recognize that thinking and composing are happening simultaneously through both these particular sign systems (Harste et al. 1984; Rowe 1994).

What needs to be equally clear, however, is that in these classrooms teachers also operate with an expanded definition of *reading*, which includes all

efforts to *express* that meaning with words or song or dance. Isabella's snow dance book, shown in Figure 6.2, actually had both words and coordinated movements to go with it when she was finished and read it to others.

Think about the fact that throughout this book we've repeatedly referred to children *reading* the books they have written. Along the way, we've captured their readings and presented them to you with accurately transcribed words because the children aren't here to read them to you. What's critical to remember, however, is that the words you see with the figures came from each child's reading and *not* vice versa; none of the children's readings came from the words. There weren't any more-accurately transcribed words in the children's books than what you see represented here. When the children read their books, the words came from their intended meanings and their best efforts to express those meanings, and their teachers respected this as reading and called it just that—*reading.*

❶ *"Snow"*

❷ *"It's a snow dance book. Let your legs up in the air with your arms up in the air."*

❸ *"One leg up in the air, one leg down, arms down low."*

❹ *"One leg straight, one leg twisted with your tongue stuck out in the snow."*

FIG. 6.2 *Isabella's Snow Dance Book*

ALREADY READY

Meet Lilly

■■■■■■■■■■■■■■■■■■■■■■■■■■■■■■■■■■■■■■

Author and Illustrator of Grocery Story

Like many of the classes at Matt's school, Lilly's was involved in a long-term study of a topic of interest—in this case, a study of grocery stores. As part of the study, the class made a site visit to the grocery store. A *site visit* for study purposes is different from a typical field trip in that it is very child-directed.

At the store, the children spent time interviewing workers about their jobs. Since they had been studying grocery stores for a while, they had lots of questions and eagerly shared their curiosity with the people there. Fortunately, the adults were happy to respond to questions, and they let the children take the lead in their study. Before leaving, they got a behind-the-scenes look at the workings of the store; and children had brought clipboards along to make sketches of what they saw inside.

Lilly is a very observant child and her attention to detail shows in her books. Because of this, she was well suited for this type of firsthand research in a setting where there was so much for her to observe. When she decided to make a book to teach people about grocery stores, her teacher realized just how much Lilly had noticed and learned from the experience.

It's easy to see how observant Lilly was during her trip by the details in her book (Figure 6.4). The first page shows one of the workers holding a lobster up to show the class members. Then, to truly appreciate this book, you need to realize that the second and third pages, and the fourth and fifth pages, are back to back and work together. The second page shows the plastic flap doorway that leads to the dairy section; when you turn the page you see what was behind the door. The store worker is placing cartons of milk into the display from the back side. The fourth and fifth pages work the same way. When you turn the page with the window in the door, you see the butcher shop. One worker is cutting meat and sliding it down the table, while the other worker is wrapping meat and sliding it into a round cart.

Like so many preschoolers' books, it would be easy to miss the level of detailed thinking in Lilly's book if you saw only the pictures and didn't hear Lilly read it and talk about what she'd illustrated. As she read this book to her friends, her intentions were so clear. Basing her book on something she'd experienced, Lilly made a book to teach people about grocery stores, and indeed, those who've read her book now find they don't go to one in quite the same way as before. They can't help but notice and think about what's going on behind all those windows and plastic flap doors in grocery stores.

① *"This is the lday showing us a lobster."*

② *"This is the door that goes to where they have the milk."*

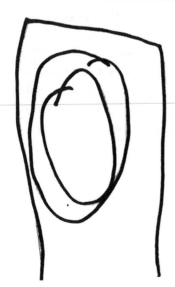

"The man is putting milk in the case." **③**

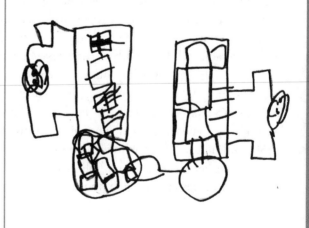

④ *"This is the door that goes to where they have the meat."*

*"One man is cutting up the meat.
The other man is wrapping it in plastic."* **⑤**

FIG. 6.4   *Lilly's Book, Grocery Story*

Supporting Young Writers Through Read-Aloud

■■■■■■■■■■■■■■■■■■■■■■■■■■■■■■

As Matt is reading Martin Waddell's *Owl Babies* to a group of preschoolers, he stops at one point and rereads a particular page. He asks the children to listen to the language Waddell has used: "Soft and silent she swooped through the trees to Sarah and Percy and Bill." Without belaboring the point, Matt says simply, "I like the way that sounds. 'Soft and silent she swooped through the trees.'" Then, he continues on with the reading. With just a tiny bit of talk inserted into the read-aloud, Matt does some important teaching. He plants seeds of understanding about how writers craft literary language, how readers are drawn to this language, and what this language sounds like in texts.

Later that morning, while Ronak is making a book about different animals, Matt helps him think about how he might make his book more interesting by telling something about each animal rather than just labeling them. Together, they think their way through the pages of the book, adding details, until they get to the last page about a snake (Figure 7.1). On this page, on his own, Ronak composes some Waddell-like text for his book when he reads, "This is a snake and it slithers and slides."

During share time, after Ronak has read his animal book to the other children, Matt gets *Owl Babies* and again reads the page he had reread earlier during read-aloud, and he comments on how much Ronak's writing sounds like Martin Waddell's writing. He also explains how Ronak revised his book to make it sound more like a book, moving from simple labels for each page to labels *and* descriptions.

This complex, connected web of teaching happened in a single day in a preschool classroom across three different predictable contexts: read-aloud, side-by-side work with a child who was writing, and share time. Day after day in each of these contexts, teachers support children's composition development as they

① *"This is an elephant. He's very big."*

② *"This is a turtle. He's very small."*

③ *"This is a giraffe. He has a long neck."*

④ *"This is a zebra. He has black-and-white stripes."*

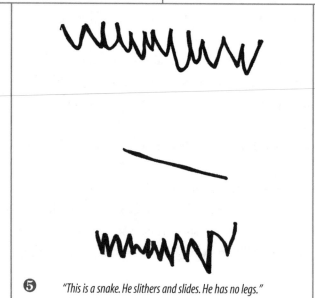

⑤ *"This is a snake. He slithers and slides. He has no legs."*

FIG. 7.1 ***Ronak's Animal Book***

use art and writing to make picture books. Teachers understand that children's development is multidimensional (Rowe 1994) and that any act of reading, writing, or sharing has the potential to lead children to multiple new understandings about texts, process, and what it means to be a writer. Think about all the different dimensions of composition development that were supported in just this one line of teaching in a single morning.

As we explained in Chapter 6, all the teaching happens in conversations with children as they read, write and share. The question, of course, is what do teachers and children talk *about* during these conversations? The purpose of this and the following chapters is to explain the kinds of talking and thinking that seem most helpful in supporting young writers. This chapter explores the talk that happens around read-alouds. As you read about this talk, remember that the intention driving it is to nudge children along in their composition development, and because this development is multidimensional, any particular instance of talk is likely to support several different dimensions at once.

Reading Aloud to Support Children as Writers

When adults share books with young children, they engage in one of the most meaningful literacy events in a child's day. Reading aloud is a complex event that involves not just reading and listening but also looking, thinking, and talking as books are shared—children and teachers making meaning together from all the rich meaning found in picture books. Of course, with preschoolers, read-aloud is also likely to be a physically interactive event, as children point and mimic and sometimes roll on the floor with laughter at the book.

With their teacher, a group of children develops a history of thinking and talking about books shared during read-aloud time, and they bring this shared history to each new reading. As a result, the literacy event changes in complexity as books are reread multiple times, as new books by familiar authors are introduced, and as new genres and topics in books are discovered.

By expanding the ways they talk with children about picture books, teachers help young writers build understandings about texts, process, and what it means to be a writer. After all, a picture book as an artifact embodies each of these facets equally: It's a text, someone went through a process to write and illustrate it, and now this person is an author who owns this book in the world. And of course, because a picture book is the same kind of writing artifact children create when they compose, the talking and thinking that happens during read-aloud is the same kind of talking and thinking that happens around children's writing. Near the end of this chapter, we'll return to this idea and consider how the talk moves seamlessly between read-aloud and children's writing.

As teachers share picture books during read-aloud, what kinds of things do they talk about with children? The following list contains five lines of thinking that teachers and children talk about, which we consider in detail in the next sections:

- The people who make books

- What makes a picture book, a picture book

- Different kinds of books

- Different purposes for books

- The decisions writers and illustrators make

Talking About the People Who Make Books

The first kind of talk teachers support and encourage is talk that helps children understand that those who make books are everyday people just like them—what we call a "concept of authorship." To better understand this concept, consider this vignette from a preschool class:

> It's read-aloud time, and the children sitting with Matt can see he has brought *Knuffle Bunny* to read to them. Matt barely gets the title out of his mouth when one of the children speaks up and says, "It's written by Mo Willems," identifying the author of this familiar book. And right on the heels of this comment, another child says, "And *Don't Let the Pigeon Ride the Bus*," naming another book by this same author.

Knowing and commenting by name—Mo Willems—on the author of a book, *and* on other books he's written, are sophisticated responses for readers of any age and experience, but they're particularly telling comments coming from preschoolers. In this case, we also find it significant that this was the *first* thing these children were thinking about when they saw a book—the person who wrote it. We know that for their thinking to have become so seamless that at the mention of a book, they think of the author, these children are in an environment where that kind of thinking is privileged and talking about authors is common, everyday talk. Their teachers understand that the concept of authorship is essential to children's images of themselves as writers.

Why? Because for young children to understand what it means for them to be writers, they first need to understand what a writer is and what a writer does.

This sounds deceptively simple, but actually it's quite complex. How many children do you know who've ever seen a writer at work? Not just an adult writing something—most of them have seen this—but an adult truly at work *making something* with writing? How many children even realize that work like this happens in the world, thinking only that books come from the store or the library?

To think of it another way, picture all the spontaneous role-playing children do in their dramatic play. The child announces, "I'm the mommy (or the doctor, the puppy, the princess, the fireman, the baby, the teacher, the waiter, etc.)," and then begins to act in the way she's seen, from experience, a mommy acts. Her sense of what it means to "be the mommy" is bounded to what she's seen mothers do. The *being* and *doing*, in other words, are very connected, and it's an easy role for her to play because she knows so much about what mommies do.

Children imagine possibilities for themselves *to be* from the range of possibilities they know exist in the world of being around them. It follows, then, that if children have had no experience with the kinds of people who make things with writing, they're not likely to imagine being writers themselves. Quite simply, they don't know what to do when it's time to "be the writer."

If very young children are to see themselves as writers, then across the year teachers must help them form a foundational understanding about the *being* and *doing* of people who write. Children need to understand that everyday, ordinary people make books by doing everyday, ordinary things—writing words and drawing pictures—and that they can make them too, if they'd like. In other words, it should be just as easy for children to imagine they can be writers as it is for them to imagine they can be mommies and daddies.

Authors and Illustrators as Familiar People

To build the critical concept of authorship, teachers surround read-aloud time with purposeful talk about the people who make books. They make it a habit to read the names of the authors and illustrators of the books they read (and reread) aloud to children. Most of the time, they read the names first, before they even read the titles, as many experienced writers often look first to see who's authored a book because they identify so strongly with authorship:

> *I have a book for you today that is written by a woman named Diane Adams. She made the words in this book and she's the author. Kevin Luthardt is the illustrator. He made the pictures. The name of their book is* Zoom.

Notice that simple definitions for *author* and *illustrator* are embedded in this talk. As teachers continue to talk about books while sharing them, they keep saying the authors' and illustrators' names as they talk, using them just as if they knew these people in person: *"I love the way Kevin drew this picture of the people on the roller coaster. Look at how he made their faces."*

Looking at photographs of the people who make books also helps children believe in them as real and familiar, not just names on a jacket cover. Many books have author and illustrator photos in them. Teachers let children look at these and talk about the people they see pictured. For books that don't have photos, teachers sometimes find them on authors' and illustrators' websites, print them, and tape them on the back covers of books.

Connected to this, teachers also read the author and illustrator blurbs on the books' back covers to see what else they can learn about these people, or they find information like this from websites. Wherever it's found, sharing personal information about authors and illustrators with children builds a concept of authorship. On the day recounted earlier when Matt brought *Knuffle Bunny* to read to the children, he also brought a photograph of Mo Willems. The children were very interested to see that Mo wears glasses just like the dad in *Knuffle Bunny*. Matt shared with them another little bit of insider information about Mo: He has a daughter named Trixie just like the Trixie in the book. In the simple act of sharing this, such important teaching happens. Children see an author as a plausibly real person, and they're exposed to a very common way that writers find ideas for writing—they use material from their own lives.

Dedications are personal little communications straight from the books' authors and illustrators. Teachers share dedications with children and wonder together about the lucky people named in them and why they were chosen. Knowing that authors have special people in their lives makes them seem more real because children understand being connected in that way. Of course, many children won't know what a dedication is, but they'll grow into understanding what one is over time the more experiences they have talking and thinking about them. Understanding that authors dedicate books to people for different reasons will also help children understand more about the powerful work writing can do in the world.

On the Importance of Rereading

The talk about authors and illustrators changes over time in ways that help strengthen children's concept of authorship. The first change happens as teachers begin to reread the same books, a highly recommended practice for how it helps support children's emergent reading, and it's just as valuable to them as writers. When teachers read a book to children for the second (or third or fourth or . . .) time, they talk about the author and illustrator like they know them, like they're familiar members of the club of people who write:

Here's that book by Diane Adams again that we liked so much—the one called Zoom—*about the roller coaster. And remember the illustrator, Kevin Luthardt, who did such a good job of showing on people's faces whether they liked the roller coaster or not?*

Rereading books deepens the concept of authorship in several ways. First, reading books again helps names and personas of authors and illustrators become familiar in the room. Talking about Eric Carle and Phyllis Root and Jon Agee should become as natural as talking about Sam and Shruthi and Miss Jenny (actual people in the room), and the naturalness of this is key to children seeing themselves as being like these authors and illustrators. Related to this, the concept of ownership and its connection to authorship is built as books are read to children multiple times. In other words, after several readings, *Zoom* isn't just a great book about roller coasters, it's also a great *Diane Adams book*.

Rereading also helps very young children understand the permanency of authorship—the idea that Diane Adams will always be the author of this book and her name will always be given in response to the question, "Who wrote this book?" The long-range implications of this understanding are significant. As children grow to be experienced writers, they'll need to understand the permanency of authorship when they put their own writing out into the world. They'll need to understand that their names will always be connected to the pieces of writing they author, and that with this comes responsibility.

Reading Multiple Books by the Same Authors and Illustrators

When children see that most writers and illustrators have published a number of books, their concept of authorship deepens. A stack of books all written and illustrated by Denise Fleming or Janet Stevens helps children understand that writing isn't a one-time event; people continue to write over time, accumulating a body of work that's associated with them as authors. They're not likely to understand this if they are always seeing new books by new authors. Then too, reading multiple books by the same authors and illustrators helps children imagine new possibilities for themselves as writers. Molly, whose book you read in Chapter 5, doesn't have to be a one-book wonder with *How Molly Became a Pirate*. She can write lots of different books that make children smile with delight, just as she wrote her pirate book. Understanding this, she might begin asking herself the same question that propels so many other writers forward, "What will I write next?"

So in addition to rereading favorite books often, teachers read multiple books by the same authors. When sharing a new book by an author whose work they've read before, teachers try to have both books with them for the read-aloud. Before reading, they spend a few minutes talking about the familiar book, and they refer to the new book in ways that indicate the author's ownership: "This is a new *George Shannon book* that you've never seen before." Over time, the stack of books grows as teachers read more and more books by the same authors.

Talking About What Makes a Picture Book, a Picture Book

The talk around read-aloud is essential to help children understand what it means, exactly, to make a picture book. Stapled blank paper and markers alone don't really help children understand what they are supposed to do in response to an invitation to make books, even though most of them will do *something* if they have paper and markers in front of them and doing something is a good place to start. But over time teachers want children to build a clearer sense of what it means to use these materials to make a book. By looking at picture books with an eye toward making them, teachers help children understand some basic things about what a picture book is and does. In conjunction with read-aloud, teachers point out a few, related essentials:

- A picture book has both words and illustrations in it.

- The words and illustrations change from page to page in a picture book (while it's still about the same topic).

- A picture book is about something, and the writer decides what this will be.

- A picture book has crafted language in it.

The first two may seem quite obvious, but teachers don't take for granted that children understand them as essential to picture book-making. They talk about these qualities of picture books often and look very specifically at them as they share books, especially early in the year when children are just beginning to make their own books.

The third essential—that picture books are about something and that writers decide what this will be—takes much longer to build as an understanding. Early in the year, teachers focus on helping children simply talk about what a book is about, and they help them see that the whole book is about the same topic. Talking about the topics of books during read-aloud helps children better understand how to answer the question, "What is your book about?" when it's asked as they're writing. Over time, this talk also helps children understand that the books they write should stay focused on a single topic.

sitting down with children and staying there long enough to observe and interact with them in thoughtful, meaningful ways, reinforcing whichever understandings and abilities make sense to support in the context of the children's play and exploration. To be clear, our vision is a teaching vision, not a management vision. In it, teachers are not simply popping in to make sure everything is okay and then moving on. Teachers are staying a while with children so that they can learn about them and teach them. This difference is important.

In classrooms where this vision is operational, making time for side-by-side teaching as children are writing is just like making time for side-by-side teaching when children are doing anything else. Teachers sit alongside children at the writing table just as they visit the dramatic play area or pull a chair up beside those who are playing musical instruments. The issue is not really so much about making time for side-by-side teaching as children are writing; the issue is believing that it matters to do so and having some idea about what that teaching might entail.

We know of two main ways teachers manage side-by-side teaching across the preschool classroom. One way is to simply move around the room with the intention of finding teaching opportunities in different children's engagements. In this case, teachers sit beside a child or a group of children and interact purposefully—posing problems, asking questions, making comments and suggestions, and sometimes showing how. These interactions typically last from five to as many as ten or fifteen minutes, depending on the energy of the interaction. A teacher who is managing her teaching this way will simply sit down beside children who are writing, as Matt did with Tashiana, and engage in side-by-side teaching. With this type of teaching, it's not uncommon for teachers to stay a while, then go away and work with other children in other places, and then return later to check in and follow up.

The other way teachers manage side-by-side teaching is to schedule blocks of time for particular activities. In this case, teachers make plans to visit a particular area or center in the room and stay there for an extended time to work with children. This is what Matt had done on the day seven children all decided to make books at the same time. Different kinds of play and exploration might be continually supported with teaching in this way, with teachers committing blocks of time for different engagements on different days.

Scheduling time to work with children who are doing particular things, such as making books, creates several opportunities. First, when children know the teacher will be staying in one place to work with them for a while, some will be motivated to become engaged in whatever the teacher is supporting and may choose an activity they wouldn't choose if the teacher wasn't there. Second, for a number of different reasons, teachers might invite specific children to work with them during a scheduled block of time, and having time set aside makes this possible.

For many teachers, making time for side-by-side teaching means balancing these two management structures. A typical day consists of some time when teachers go out and find teaching opportunities, and some scheduled time when they support children's engagements more specifically.

The Difference Between Nudging and Pushing

When working side-by-side with young writers, teachers want to nudge development along, not push it or force it. The goal of the teaching, in addition to moving development forward, is to leave children with energy and enthusiasm for the whole idea of making books. After all, if children don't come back to the table to write again, then they won't have this context in which they can continue to grow as writers. So teachers think about the future of their teaching, as well as the now of it, and focus on giving children gentle nudges that are proximal to their existing development.

Often, there is a fine line between a nudge and a push, between what gives a child energy and what takes it away. The line can be drawn differently for different children, and even differently for the same children on different days. Because of this, teachers must be close observers as they work side-by-side with children, monitoring all kinds of verbal cues and body language for signs that they are happy and comfortable with the direction of the interaction. If a child seems frustrated by the questions the teacher is asking or the suggestions being made, then most likely the line has been crossed from a nudge to a push.

Matt realized he'd crossed this line as he worked with Hunter one afternoon. As Matt approached the table, he could see that Hunter was energetically going at his writing, and that's very much what it looked like—he was *going at it*. There were sound effects and body movements accompanying most every action he took to put something on paper. Matt asked Hunter about the first page of his book, which was already full of illustrations, and Hunter pointed to his pictures and labeled them: Zorro, a Jurassic Park school, battle stations, a tornado. Then with a sudden burst of marking, he added something to the illustration; when Matt asked what it was, Hunter said, "It's lines."

As they turned to the second page, Matt asked Hunter to think ahead about what would go on the blank page. "Jurassic Park," was the answer, and then Matt asked what he would need to draw for this. With some nudging, Hunter said he would need a river, some trees, a house, and a dinosaur. It was clear from his tone and posture, however, that he was losing the energy he had for writing before Matt sat down. As he began to draw the dinosaur, Matt asked leading questions designed to help Hunter clarify the meaning of his illustration, and Hunter added eyes, teeth, and a long tail to the dinosaur. But after these additions on just the second page, Hunter declared himself "all done with this Jurassic Park." He got up to leave the table, clearly deciding he was no longer interested in finishing the book he had started. Matt let him go, of course, practicing the fine art of this teaching—knowing when to let go and being willing to do so.

As teachers get to know more and more about individual children, their interaction styles and their learning styles, they can better anticipate what the boundary will be between nudging and pushing. Of course, as teachers learn more about what children already know and can do as writers, they can direct their interactions more purposefully toward a particular child's zone of proximal development, increasing the likelihood their assistance will be taken as a nudge and not a push. The key, once again, is to engage the child in talking and thinking about writing in ways that nudge composition development, while maintaining the energy and enthusiasm for writing the child had when he or she chose to make a book.

Related to this, teachers must be thoughtful about when they are talking too much as a child is writing. The point is not to ask question after question; the point is to watch and listen—sometimes observing for quite a while before saying anything. Then engage the child in just a little talking and thinking that makes sense in the context of his or her actions. If a teacher senses that an interaction feels more forced than natural and responsive, he or she should step away and allow the child to regain control of the engagement in writing.

Helping Children Believe in Their Abilities as Writers

Another issue that impacts so much side-by-side teaching with young writers, especially when they're just getting started, is helping them believe in their own abilities. While not a specific dimension of composition development, a growing confidence in one's ability to make something with writing is essential to all other development. Knowing that children must be helped to see themselves as capable makers of books, what do teachers say in response when children share their doubts? "I don't know how to draw a car" or "I'm not sure about putting in words." How do teachers help children believe they can do things preschoolers doubt they can do?

While working on a book about his teacher, three-year-old Matthew told Matt he didn't know how to draw an ear, though he wanted to add one to his picture of Miss Jenny. Matt responded by asking him what an ear looks like. Matthew studied Matt's ear for a moment, and then he said, "It kind of looks like two bumps and a line across it." Matt said, "Well. I wonder if you could draw it like that." Looking at an ear and describing it seemed to demystify the idea of drawing one, so Matthew took his pencil and quickly added an ear to his illustration. As soon as he was finished, he asked Matt, "Does that look like an ear?" Matt replied, "I think so. I think it looks just like a three-year-old would draw an ear."

Some version of this sort of exchange is played out often in interactions with children who are writing, and this particular vignette shows Matt following two of the most common lines of thinking. First, he figures out what sensible assistance he might give based on a child's current development. Second, he supports the simple but critical understanding that being capable means working as best you can with what you've got. After all, when you're three and drawing an ear, what should you reasonably expect that ear to look like when you're finished?

Helping children have reasonable expectations for the finished products of their writing is essential to helping them see themselves as capable. Matt often says to children when he's working with them, "You're four years old. Just do it the best you can." And when he says this, he doesn't mean that because of their inexperience it doesn't make any difference how they write. Matt's just reminding them that they have to write within their abilities—this is all that's being asked of them; it's perfectly acceptable for their writing to look like it was done by three- and four-year-old writers. It's okay for Matthew's ear illustration to look *ear-ish*, as the wonderful picture book *Ish* by Peter Reynolds teaches us. After all, if young writers aren't comfortable with their approximations, they'll be tentative at best, and some won't try to write anything at all.

Teachers understand that once children are comfortable with their approximations and are willing to write and illustrate as best they can, their questions about how to do things won't stop. Children will continue to encounter new kinds of things as they write and illustrate, and how teachers respond to them during these times has everything to do with their overall confidence as writers. For example, in this same interaction with Matthew, on his own he wrote the first five letters of his name and then said to Matt, "I'm not sure how to make the *e*." Seeing his confidence in writing the other letters, Matt knew Matthew wasn't afraid to try to write his name. Clearly the *e* just perplexed him in a way the other letters didn't, so Matt got a name card with Matthew's name on it and they studied the *e* together and then practiced making the letter several times.

With this response, Matt made a very different decision about what would best support him than he did earlier when Matthew expressed doubts about drawing an ear. The bottom line is: There is no always-right answer to what should happen when teachers sit with children who are writing. Development is complex and rarely linear, and children often surprise us. This leads to a final point to consider about side-by-side teaching: understanding teaching as responsive action.

Teaching as a Responsive Action

With a solid understanding of composition development as a guide, teachers sitting beside those who are making books will find many opportunities to "teach into" children's actions. Using the questions related to composition development as a lens for assessment, teachers watch children and listen to them closely, searching for sensible ways to nudge them as they grow their understandings about texts, process, and what it means to be a writer. To know how to nudge, however, it's very important that teachers have a clear sense of what they're nudging *toward*; such a clear sense comes from understanding the curricular implications of assessment.

Table 8.1 lists the assessment questions that frame each dimension of composition development, then reframes each one and states it as curriculum. Teaching—nudging—is the bridge between assessment and curriculum, and understanding curriculum helps teachers know what they're nudging toward as they work side-by-side with children who are making books.

In truth, all the curriculum spelled out in the table is the same curriculum needed by writers of any age. The only difference for preschool writers is that it must be understood in developmentally appropriate ways in the context of three- and four-year-olds' writing. This is why we first defined composition development in Chapter 4 through an assessment lens rather than a curricular lens. Teachers cannot plan ahead for the teaching they'll do in side-by-side interactions because such teaching must happen in response to children's actions; therefore, having an operational "big picture" understanding of assessment and curriculum is critical. As Katie explains in her book *The Writing Workshop* (2001):

> When we sit down next to a student, we bring with us what I call a "fistful" of knowledge about writing that we draw from to teach this writer. And in a conference, we can't teach what we don't know. We can teach what we don't know in a lesson we plan for next Friday because we can read up on it and get to know it. But in a conference, all we've got to go on is what's already in our fist because we have to do it right there on the spot. (164)

TABLE 8.1 Assessment Questions That Frame Composition Development's Dimensions

ASSESSMENT	CURRICULUM
Understandings About Texts	
Is the child's book *about* something?	Writers focus on a topic when they compose a text.
How has the child organized this book? What is the connection between ideas?	The ideas in a text should be organized in logical ways.
When the child reads the book, does it sound like a book?	The language in written texts has been crafted in particular ways.
Does the child read the book in basically the same way over time?	The symbols (words and illustrations) in texts hold consistent meaning over time.
Is the child making the book *in the manner* of other picture books he or she has seen?	Different publishing formats have particular features writers use to make meaning.
What does this book show the child understands about genre?	Different kinds of writing in the world serve different purposes for different audiences and have features in common that readers expect.
How is the child representing meaning in this book?	Writers use both illustrations (graphics and layout) and written text to make meaning.
Understandings About Process	
Is the child being intentional about what she or he is representing on the page?	Writers are purposeful and engage in a continuous process of decision making as they compose texts.
Does the child engage in revision while composing the picture book?	Writers make changes to clarify meaning, enhance style, make texts more readable, and so on.
Is there any evidence the child is thinking ahead about what to write next?	Writers think ahead as they compose, keeping the text as a whole in mind.
Has the child made any intentional crafting decisions in the book?	Writers often use crafting techniques to make their texts more engaging for readers.
How long has the child worked on this book? In one sitting? Over time?	Writers must stick to the task of writing to see a text through to completion (stamina).
Does the child exhibit a willingness to solve problems while writing?	Writers must be problem solvers.
Understandings About What It Means to Be a Writer	
How (and why) has the child decided to write this book?	Writers choose meaningful topics (or find meaning in assigned topics) and write for purposeful reasons.
How interested is the child in an audience's response to the book?	Writing that is made public will be read, and writers are often mindful of potential readers as they compose.
Has the child composed in a way that led to new meaning as he or she was writing?	Composing often helps writers find new meaning in the process of expressing existing meaning.
Does the book show that the child has been willing to take compositional risks?	Writers often find aspects of composing to be very challenging.
As I interact with this child around this book, does he or she seem to have a sense of self as a writer? A sense of history?	Over time, writers come to know themselves in this particular way (as writers) based on their experiences.
Does the child show an understanding of his or her powerful position as the author of the book?	Writers are responsible for the words they put into the world.

The good thing is, most preschool teachers are much more in tune with teaching as responsive action than teachers of older children. After all, preschool classrooms are active places where teachers must go out and find teaching opportunities. In side-by-side work with young writers, then, the teaching act itself is a familiar one. What is no doubt new for some teachers is the particular knowledge base about writing, and especially writing as composition, that informs this teaching.

"Filling one's fist" with understandings about writing will help teachers have more and more confidence every time they sit down next to children who are making books. It may be that after reading this book, you will be interested in growing your own knowledge base about writing even more. If you are, a short, select list of some books you might find helpful follows. All are written with much more-experienced writers in mind, but again, the understandings they build about writing are not bound by development. If a teacher like Matt truly believes a four-year-old like Tashiana is a writer, then when he sits next to her, Matt needs to know *What a Writer Needs*—the title of one of the valuable resources on this list.

Books to Improve Teachers' Knowledge Base About Writing

Bird by Bird: Some Instructions on Writing and Life by Anne Lamott

Crafting Authentic Voice by Tom Romano

Live Writing: Breathing Life into Your Words by Ralph Fletcher

On Writing Well by William Zinsser

Steering the Craft by Ursula Le Guin

Take Joy: A Book for Writers by Jane Yolen

The Muses Among Us: Eloquent Listening and Other Pleasures of the Writer's Craft by Kim Stafford

What a Writer Needs by Ralph Fletcher

Writing Down the Bones: Freeing the Writer Within by Natalie Goldberg

Writing Toward Home by Georgia Heard

Meet Mary Catherine

■■■■■■■■■■■■■■■■■■■■■■■■■■■■■■■■■■■■■

Author and Illustrator of How to Make Pudding

Activities involving cooking and food are common in many preschool classrooms. On the day Mary Catherine made her *How to Make Pudding* book, her class had worked together to make pumpkin pudding. By the time Matt arrived, the children were sitting down to enjoy their pudding. Since he wasn't there when they made it, Matt asked questions about the cooking process.

Mary Catherine and her friends told him how they mixed the ingredients together and added the spices. They shared how they took turns stirring, and who liked the taste and who didn't. Matt asked questions about what they did first, and then second. He asked about important things to remember when making pudding. The children were glad to share their expertise.

Thinking aloud, Matt said he thought his daughters might like to make pumpkin pudding and that if he had a book about making pudding, he could read it to Molly and Natalie. He added, "If anyone decides to make a book about making pudding, be sure to let me know." Knowing how easily they'd been able to talk about making pudding, he wasn't surprised when several children decided to make books about the process. Several books shared the basic steps of making pudding, with illustrations showing children holding the bowl, adding milk, and so on.

Mary Catherine took a different approach with her book. Rather than drawing a whole person, she was very intentional in her decision to just show the hands and the bowl, or the hands and the ingredients, like you might see in a cookbook for adults. When asked, Mary Catherine said she wasn't sure if she'd seen these types of illustrations before. Either way, her illustrations are the result of interesting thinking and specific intention.

The last page of *How to Make Pudding* shows a cup of pudding and a hand with a spoon. Above the bowl, two mouths are pictured. Mary Catherine explained that the round one is her open mouth getting ready for the pudding, and the other one is her closed mouth as she is chewing. To make sure he understood, Matt asked Mary Catherine where she would put her eyes (in relation to the mouths) if she chose to add them to her picture. With great tolerance for such an obvious question, Mary Catherine pointed to a spot on the table just above the paper, exactly where the eyes would need to be if she had chosen to draw that type of picture.

Mary Catherine has some letter–sound knowledge, so it was appropriate for her to say some words slowly and write the sounds she heard. She wrote two *s*'s for *spices* and an *m* for *milk*. She also wrote the names of people she was planning to read her book to, and since she's an avid mailer of letters, she added a stamp above their names.

In this book Mary Catherine benefited from a classroom environment that didn't provide a preset, fill-in-the-blank way of making a book. The decision making she engaged in as she composed *How to Make Pudding* shows not just what she knows about pudding, but more important, it also shows the interesting way she sees and thinks about her world.

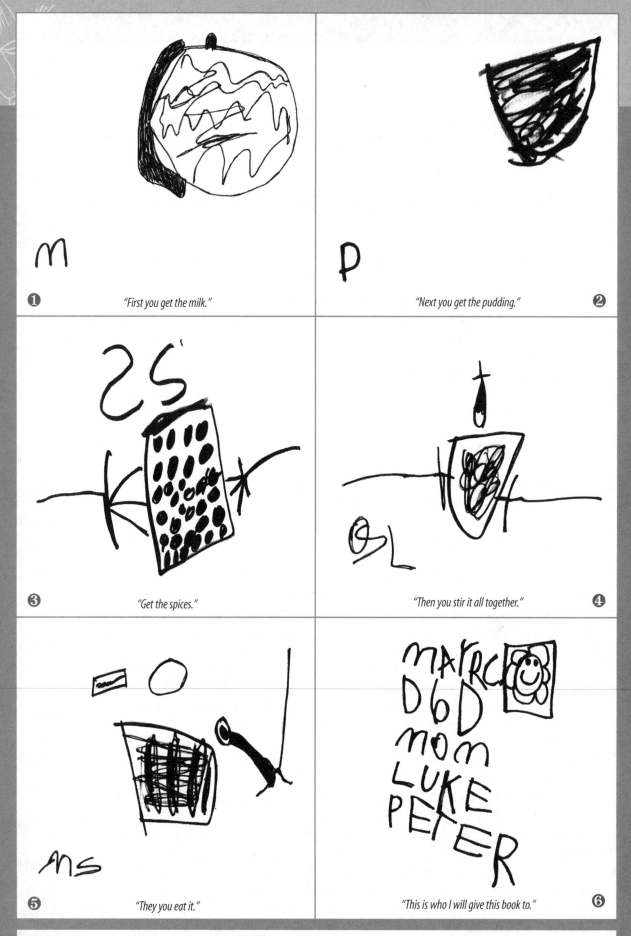

M

① "First you get the milk."

P

② "Next you get the pudding."

③ "Get the spices."

④ "Then you stir it all together."

⑤ "They you eat it."

⑥ "This is who I will give this book to."

FIG. 8.1 *Mary Catherine's Book*, **How to Make Pudding**

Building a Repertoire of Responsive Actions for Side-by-Side Teaching

■■■■■■■■■■■■■■■■■■■■■■■■■■■■■■■■■■■■■

Over time, as teachers sit next to children who are making books at crowded and sometimes not-so-crowded tables, they develop a repertoire of responsive actions that make sense in the context of children's book-making and support a range of composition development. Crafting a particular interaction from this repertoire requires teachers to select their teaching responses thoughtfully and not to take over children's writing with too much talk.

The question is: What are the kinds of things teachers say and do as they sit beside young children who are making books? What does it mean to have a "repertoire of responsive actions" from which a thoughtful teaching interaction can be crafted? Throughout this book, you've "listened in" on a number of these interactions as we've told stories about Matt working alongside young writers. In this chapter, we describe this teaching repertoire a little more explicitly by naming some of the teaching moves Matt and other preschool teachers make as they work with children. As you read about this teaching, please keep the understandings built in Chapter 8 present in your thinking:

- @ How teachers make time for side-by-side teaching

- @ The difference between nudging children and pushing them

- @ The importance of helping children believe in their own abilities as writers

- @ The nature of teaching as responsive action

A Repertoire of Responses and Actions

Building Ideas: Talking About What Books Are About

"What is your book about?" is one of the most common questions teachers ask as they interact with young writers. In asking this question, teachers hope to get children talking about the ideas they are trying to represent in their books. From the talk around ideas, teachers can nurture so much thinking about composition. For example, if a child says her book is about trains, imagine all the different ways a teacher can engage her in talk that will help her thinking grow. The teacher and the child might:

- talk about what the child knows about trains, helping her understand the fullness of the topic and how much she has to bring to a book as an author with some expertise.

- imagine what ideas—all of them about trains—could stretch across the pages, if the child is just starting on the book and they are blank.

- think about what kind of book she's writing about trains. Is it a story about trains, or is it a list book that tells about trains? Might she add some features like she's seen in other books? If so, what might make sense with the trains topic? A close-up view of a train? A map with a train on it?

- consider how this book about trains is similar and different from other books she's written.

- use their talk to revise the book, adding things to the illustrations or words that make the meanings clearer. The child's talk about the topic is always bigger than what's represented on the paper, so there are many opportunities to engage in thinking about revision. For example, the child might add windows with people inside if she says people are riding on the train. If the child has a marker in her hand, she will likely engage in this kind of revision spontaneously while talking.

In many ways, the talk around what a book is about is a rehearsal for the writing, especially if the conversation happens when the child is just setting out to write or before he's finishing. The talking helps the child imagine possibilities for what he might represent next in the book.

Talking with a child about what a book is about may seem like a simple enough interaction, and certainly many children will begin talking about what they are drawing or writing the moment someone is within earshot. Such children sort of narrate their writing as they are in the act of composing it. But teachers also need to be prepared for a variety of issues they may encounter when trying to engage children in this talk.

First, teachers should realize that the question itself, "What is your book *about*?" will be something new for many children, and they may not know exactly what you are asking. After all, *about* is a conceptual idea, not a concrete one, and many children will not have encountered the *about* concept in other contexts. If children seem confused by the question, here are some other entry points into this important conversation you might try.

- ✺ If there is anything on the paper, ask the child to tell you about what she's drawn or written. Many children don't understand the question, "What is *your book* about?" at first, but they have no problem talking about what they've got on the paper. If the child points to her illustration and says, "It's a girl and a flower," then you might say this back to her as, "So this is *a book* about a girl and a flower." The child needs to hear the word *about* used in context to come to understand it.

- ✺ If you have been talking about what books are about during read-aloud time, you might refer to that talk to help the child understand your question. You can say, "You know how *Zoom!* is all *about* people on a roller coaster, and *Owl Babies* is all *about* the owls wanting their mommy? What is your book going to be all *about*?"

- ✺ If the child has something on the paper, but doesn't seem to know how to talk about it, you might name what you see: "It looks like you've drawn a big sun there." Just this small bit of naming often gets a child talking about what's represented there.

- ✺ If you don't have any idea what the illustration is meant to represent, try just naming the colors and features of what you see. "My, it's very purple and has lines swirling all around." Similarly, this small bit of talk often helps the child start talking about what's on the paper—"Yes, it's my necklace." Of course, sometimes the child has just taken a purple marker and made swirls on the paper, not intending to really represent anything. In this case, just naming it as purple and swirly helps build the important understanding that what's on the paper can be talked about and is representative of something.

- ✺ Sometimes the child tells you what is represented on each page, but the topic changes and the book is not really about any one thing. You might try finding some common link between the ideas and naming it for the child. For example, if page one has a bicycle, page two an ice cream cone, page three a baby sister, and page four a butterfly, you might ask, "Are these all things that you like?" If the answer is yes, then you might say, "So this is a book all about things you like." The child probably wasn't intending to write a book about things she likes, but by naming it this way, you are showing her that ideas in a book should be connected somehow.

Engaging in Process: Talking About How Children Are Writing

Sometimes the talk around writing is process talk as teachers and children think together about how they are going about their writing. This talk is critical because it builds beginning understandings about writing as a process, introduces children to some language to talk about process, and helps them work with more intention as they take their next steps in writing. Much of the talk around process grows from close observations of children as they're writing. The teacher's primary role is to notice what a child is doing while writing, and then to call attention to the "moves" being made as he or she composes. To give you a feel for this, here are some examples of things children might do that you could name as process for them.

- If a child announces what he is getting ready to draw before drawing it, you might say, "That's smart how you're thinking ahead about your idea before you even put anything on the paper."

- If a child looks ahead at the blank pages in the book, or looks back at the pages already finished, you might say, "I noticed how you are thinking about how your book might go by looking to see how many pages you have." Or in the case of looking back, "I think it's smart that you're going back and reading what you've got so far. This will help you decide what comes next."

- If a child adds something to the illustrations while talking about what's pictured there, you might say, "Look how you revised that—you added that into your picture and now I can see what you mean so much better."

- If a child adds some writing to a page that's fully illustrated, you might say, "I noticed that you illustrate first and then write your words. I bet the pictures help you think about what words you need." Some children, of course, will start with writing and then add illustrations, so this opposite process can be pointed out as well: "I noticed that you do your writing first and then draw what you need to go with that writing."

⊘ If a child gets a different color marker to make the writing (after illustrating), you might say, "That's interesting how you used different color markers for the illustrations and the writing. It shows that your words and pictures are two different parts."

Noticing what children are doing and naming it for them is a very common way of teaching about process, and anything a teacher sees children doing that moves their writing forward can be considered part of the process. Teachers also ask children questions to initiate talking and thinking about process. Here are some examples of questions you can ask children about process.

⊘ "What are you going to do first?" Or, "What are you going to do next?" Questions like these nudge children to think ahead about what their next moves will be and make them with more intention.

⊘ "Where did you get the idea for this book?" This question helps children understand that writers have reasons for writing about the topics they choose.

⊘ "That's so interesting. Why did you decide to <u>make the dog's head so big in this picture?</u>" By filling in the underlined part of this question with anything you see that is interesting in the child's book, you've planted the idea that writers make decisions about how they craft texts.

⊘ "How long have you been making this book?" This question helps children think about their work as a product developed over time.

⊘ "What are you thinking about?" You might ask this question of a child who has stopped and is clearly thinking in the midst of making a book.

Basically any question that gets a child talking about what he or she is doing or thinking about while writing holds important teaching potential. Here's the thing about questions like these: Teachers know that sometimes they won't get any response to them, or they'll get responses that don't make much sense in the context of the question. But simply hearing the questions does important teaching work because it helps children begin to see themselves as people who ought to have answers to questions like these, since teachers keep asking them. The questions also plant seeds of things for children to think about as they write that can grow over time.

Related to this, teachers shouldn't shy away from the words or concepts that they need to talk with children about process. Some of the language will be unfamiliar, but encountering it in familiar contexts over time is what will help children learn to talk as writers. A good example of this is the expression "so far." As Matt is working with children who are in the middle of making a book, he will often say to them, "Let's see what you've got *so far*." With some children, it's clear that this process language and the concept of *so far*—indicating an ongoing state of the writing—is unfamiliar. Rather than shy away from this conceptual language, however, Matt simply helps children understand what it means to be in the middle of something and to see what they have "so far" by showing them how to take their books and go back to the first pages and talk about what's there.

Sometimes as teachers observe those who are making books, they offer suggestions or strategies for the issues children encounter in the process of writing. On the day Matt sat with the seven children who were writing, he helped Lilly with a very big process issue she faced with her writing. When Lilly looked at the two pages she had "so far" in her Build-a-Bear Workshop® book, she realized that on just the second page she had the bears already completely finished. This presented a problem because completed bears is really the end of the story she wanted to relate. Matt could tell she sensed this from the way she shared what she had with him, so he offered her two options. He suggested she might continue the story with what she and her sister did with the bears after they took them home, or, he explained, they could take the staples out of the book and move that page to the end; then she could write about how they actually made the bears at the workshop. Lilly chose the second option, and Matt helped her with the mechanics of removing the staples and moving the page (Figure 9.1).

All sorts of process issues can arise as children are making books—how to add things in, take things out, move things around, think of more ideas, make things clearer, and sometimes even how to start over. Usually the process issue presents itself in the child's talk as in, "This doesn't go here" or "Wait, I need to show him being mad." Often children solve process issues all on their own, and when they do, teachers want to call attention to that problem solving and confirm its smartness. But when children don't seem to know how to solve a process issue they've encountered, teachers need to offer them process strategies as Matt did with Lilly.

Grabbing Hold of Meanings: The Importance of Repetition

When working with young writers, it is important for teachers to repeat most everything children say about the meanings they are making as they compose. After all, some of the illustrating and much of the writing will not be represen-

FIG. 9.1   *Lilly's Book About the Build-a-Bear Workshop®*

tational, so the process of layering in lots of repetition helps children grab hold of their meanings and begin to keep them constant.

Although it might seem awkward at first, teachers get in the habit of repeating most everything children are saying as they're writing. When a child spontaneously narrates what she's composing, the teacher repeats a lot of what the child says as they interact. "I am going to draw my daddy," she says, and the teacher says, "You're going to draw your daddy." When the drawing is finished, the teacher repeats it again, "This is your daddy."

When a teacher asks a child a question and he or she responds, it's important for the teacher to repeat the response as well. For example, when Matt asked Ida why Peter Pan has a rock on his head in her book about Tinker Bell, Ida said, "It's because Peter Pan is silly." Hearing this, Matt said, "Look at that silly Peter Pan with a rock on his head," repeating the idea of her response, but changing it a little so that it was a more natural response to what she'd said.

Again, the key with all this repetitive talk is that it supports children in holding their meanings constant over time. Repetition also helps them remember the language they've crafted for their texts. When one young writer says that Venom is the "baddest bad guy of all" in his Spiderman book, Matt wants him to hold on to this crafty language, so Matt is careful to repeat the phrase often as they talk and interact around the book.

Helping Children Learn to Read Their Books

Perhaps the most significant side-by-side work teachers do with young writers is to help them learn to read the books they're making. The key in this work is helping children hear and understand the difference between talking about a book (spontaneous words) and reading a book (crafted words). A simple interaction between Matt and Jewel will illustrate the most common way teachers help children understand this difference between talking and reading. Matt asked Jewel to tell him about the page in her book you see in Figure 9.2. Jewel pointed to her pictures and labeled them: "This is a monkey. And this is an orange and a banana." Matt asked her why she'd drawn an orange and a banana and Jewel said, "Because that's what monkeys eat." Matt took the simple threads of this idea and said, "Okay then, let me read this page to you like it's a page in a book. *The monkey is eating an orange and a banana.*"

The teaching move is to take the central idea represented in the child's talk and craft it so that it sounds the way the words might sound in a book. The dif-

FIG. 9.2 *A Page from Jewel's Book About Animals*

ference is subtle, but distinct, and many children will need lots of experience hearing teachers take their talk and craft it into reading as they learn to do this on their own. Figure 9.3 shows three sample pages from children's books, the language each child used to talk about the pages, and a possible reading a teacher might demonstrate from that talk.

Several common teaching moves are captured in these possible readings. The first move in reading a child's book is simply to take all that's been said about a page and say it again in a connected way without interruption. Sometimes there have been several minutes of talk about a single page before the teacher stops, brings it all together, and reads the page back to the child. Another move is take the child's idea and enrich the language just a tiny bit, as in using the word *pouring* for the rain since it's clear from the illustration there is lots of rain coming down, or using the word *shelf* to name the "place inside the oven."

Attending to the genre of the writing also helps the teacher craft the reading, as you can see so clearly in the *How to Make Cinnamon Biscuits* reading, which sounds like how-to language. Finally, teachers sometimes use literary sentence constructions when it makes sense to; the phrase, *As the rain came pouring down,* allows children to hear language used in a book-way rather than an everyday-talking-way.

What's critical in teaching children to read their books is helping them hear new language possibilities for the meanings they want to represent. We should be very clear that teachers aren't trying to change children's meanings, not at all; there is no insistence either that children read their books the same way the teacher reads them. Teachers simply are helping children hear their books differently, providing an important demonstration of what it means to craft words in particular ways.

When demonstrating for children how to read their books, repetition is very important. If a teacher is working side by side with a child and the goal is to teach him or her to read the book, then the teacher needs to go back and read the pages they've crafted together more than once. When Matt is working in this way with children, he'll often say, "Let me see if I've got this right" as he rereads and they frequently correct him when he doesn't! As teachers are engaged in this sort of interaction, they sometimes make personal notes to capture some of the reading's essential language to help them remember it.

Assessing Children's Book Reading Is Critical

Assessment in this particular aspect of teaching is really important because the goal is for children to become comfortable reading their books on their own and to know what to do when someone asks, "Will you read me your book?" As a matter of fact, before a teacher even demonstrates the move from talking about

Mitchell's Band Book

Pointing to the various sets of eyes, Mitchell says that this is his band. Nolan is playing the drums, he (Mitchell) is playing the guitar, and Justin is playing the piano. He explains that it's loud and the scattered marks represent the sound all around. A possible reading: *Mitchell, Nolan, and Justin are in a band—Mitchell on guitar, Nolan on the drums, and Justin on piano. They play loudly, and the sound is all around them.*

How to Make Cinnamon
Biscuits *by Maddie and*
Justin

Maddie and Justin first label their pictures—a pan with all the biscuits, an oven with a handle on it, and "a place for you to put the biscuits inside the oven." They then explain that "You have to let Ms. Cheryl put the biscuits in because it's hot." A possible reading: *Next you line up all the biscuits on a pan and wait for the oven to get very hot inside. Find an adult to help you, and then carefully place the pan of biscuits on the shelf inside.*

Mackenzie's Book
About a Party

Mackenzie explains that her mother is inside the house, and she's making a cake for a party. The blue triangles are the rain falling down. A possible reading: *As the rain came pouring down, Mommy was inside the house making a cake for the party.*

FIG. 9.3 **Possible Readings of Children's Books**

a book to reading a book, it's a good idea to first see what the child will do in response to the request to read it. If the child naturally reads it so it sounds like a book, then the teacher should go with that reading and simply support it, rereading it often to keep it constant for the child.

When Matt asked Kara to read her completed book about zoo animals to him, she said she needed a few minutes to think about what the words should be. He waited and watched as she looked through her pages, and when she was ready, she read it to him (see Figure 9.4).

Kara's actions and reading clearly showed she didn't need Matt to demonstrate how her book might be read. She read the list book in the manner of other list books, repeating the basic sentence structure and idea for each animal (what that animal is doing). Her request to have some time to think about what the words should be showed she understood that reading a book required thinking about what she'd say in a way simply talking about a book would not.

❶ *"The giraffe is eating leaves."*

"The wolf is rounding up his food and eating it." ❷

❸ *"The lion is growling on the rocks."*

"The bears are playing hide-and-go-seek behind the rocks." ❹

FIG. 9.4 *Kara's Zoo Animals Book*

One response teachers sometimes encounter when they ask a child to read his book is, "I can't read it. There aren't any words there." Without a doubt this response indicates the child knows that print is what people typically read when they think of reading, but it also shows that he is operating with a limited view of reading. If a child says this, the teacher might suggest adding some writing and then reading the book.

Some children will take this nudge and immediately add some sort of writing, but some will be more reluctant. If a child doesn't seem ready to add writing, the teacher can simply respond, "Well, if there were words there, what would they say?" This comment often nudges children to read their books. If it doesn't, teachers know they need to demonstrate for children how books like those they've composed can be read.

When Words Are Present

With most preschoolers, teachers will be dealing with writing that ranges from linear, letter-like marks, to random strings of letters, to some sound–symbol letters representing key words in the idea on a page. The readings of these books will come from the illustrations and the talk around them as we've already explained. But some children will cross over into writing that is clearly representational and can be used to read the books they compose. Figures 9.5 and 9.6 show two such books written by four-year-olds.

When children are at this point in their transcription development, teachers need to help them learn to read the actual words they've written on the page. Just because children have written something doesn't mean the words are easy for them to read. For a while, children often actually outwrite themselves as readers. They know how to do the thinking that leads to spelling, but thinking at the individual letter level is not the same thinking they'll need for reading whole words and sentences. Also, children may be spelling quite well while still approximating letter formation and word spacing, adding additional challenges to reading their written texts again. This kind of approximation is evident in both of the following samples.

Teachers working with children at this point in their transcription development continue to operate with an expanded definition of *reading*. Children's ideas are going to be much bigger than what they can realistically represent through transcription, so if teachers want to support continued composition development, they need to capture the fullness of these ideas. When it's clear there is a lot more happening in an illustration than a child has been able to represent through transcription, the teacher can show him or her how to read the written text first, and then how to add to that reading by composing text to go with the illustration and the meaning captured in it.

FIG. 9.5 **Pranav's Book About the Solar System**

"Solar System"

FIG. 9.5 *Continued*

Nudging Toward Print

If young writers are making books and using only illustrations to hold their meanings, teachers will want to nudge these children to add writing to their books. Of course, whatever a child understands about print is what will qualify as writing in the book. As we've explained before, these understandings about print will range from what looks like linear scribbles, to letter-like symbols, to random actual letters, to letters that represent key sounds in words, to invented spellings that represent particular words. In just the examples included in this chapter, that entire range of understandings about print is represented.

ALREADY READY

FIG. 9.6 *Colin's Soccer Game Book*

Teachers should not assume that children who haven't used any writing in their books don't know much about print. Many children know lots about print but simply don't use the knowledge, unless nudged to use it, because drawing is their first, more natural response to meaning-making on paper. This is why it's important to start nudging children to put writing (of any form) in their books early on as they make them so that teachers can assess what they understand about print at this point in their development. Additionally, if children are encouraged to use writing with illustrating every time they make a book, their transcription development will have a context in which it can grow and thrive over time.

Here are some suggestions that might be helpful as you work side by side with children and encourage them to use writing in their books.

- Remember that you're not asking for writing that is *right*. You simply want the child to use whatever thinking he has about what writing is and what writing does to use it in books. In most cases, whatever a child does in response to your request to add writing should be treated as a successful "go" at adding writing.

- The simplest way to nudge a child to add writing is to say, "Do you think you could add some writing to this page?" This request is best positioned after some talk about what is represented in the illustration. You may have to support the child to believe in her ability to add writing, as we discussed earlier, and help her understand that you just want her to do it the best she can.

- One way you might frame the nudge to add writing is to remind the child that the books you share during read-aloud, which are like what he is making, have both pictures and words in them.

- Be mindful of moving from nudging to pushing when encouraging children to add writing to their books. For example, if adding writing to the book is something very new to a child and she is tentative about it at best, you may decide to suggest adding writing to just the cover or one or two pages rather than the whole book. If a child is clearly uncomfortable with the idea of writing at all, you can always step away and hold the suggestion for another time.

Once children are using writing a lot in their books, they'll show you when they are ready to be helped with some basic understandings about transcription, and then you'll begin to nudge in different ways. For example, unlike many of his preschool classmates, Colin is far enough along in his development that he is ready to learn about spacing between words—and how much spacing makes

"Spiderman. Venom."

FIG. 9.7 *Asher's page shows him and Spiderman fighting Venom.*

rereading easier—because his writing shows a clear sense of "wordedness" (see Figure 9.6).

Observation is so critical in knowing what makes sense to support in children's transcription development. For example, by just looking at a page from Asher's book about Spiderman in Figure 9.7, you might think he is using random strings of letters for his writing. But because Matt was there and saw him write on this page, he knows that Asher actually used fairly sophisticated sound–symbol knowledge to write the letters for *Spiderman* and *Venom*.

As Matt watched, Asher said the two words very slowly, actually segmenting them into the sounds he heard, using a very sophisticated spelling strategy. When he decided on a letter, he wrote it wherever he could find to put it on the page. The letters look very random, when actually they were very intentionally generated. Asher is ready to be helped to understand how the letters in a word are written from left to right and how they go together on a page. Although it may take lots of time for him to really grasp this idea, the time to start nudging toward it is now. Just as with all other composition development, teachers have to be careful about thinking of certain writing "skills" as being the teaching domain of later schooling. Children are ready to learn what they show us they are ready to learn, and perhaps nowhere is this more evident than in the development of understandings about transcription.

Having said so much about nudging children to add writing to their books, occasionally teachers will need to nudge them to add illustrations to books. Gavin wrote and shared his book about a race car with his preschool class

FIG. 9.8 *Gavin's Book About a Race Car*

(Figure 9.8), and all the pages but the last one have *only* writing on them. The last page shows the motion of the race car zooming around the track.

Children who use mostly writing in a book often have no problem reading their books, but the meanings are likely to vary significantly from one reading to the next. Without illustrations, there are no representative meaning clues to serve as reminders, making it more difficult for the child to hold meaning constant.

One Child, So Many Possibilities

Perhaps the greatest challenge teachers of young writers face is the fine art of selection because, in a single interaction with a child who is making a book, so many nudging points are possible. Deciding which points to pursue and when enough is enough is part of the art of teaching writing (Calkins 1994). In practically every piece of writing presented in this chapter, you no doubt can see other ways each child might have been nudged. But remember that the goal is to teach the writer, not the writing, and just a small teaching nudge is the goal. After all, a single interaction with a child is only one stop on a long, long journey as he or she grows into an experienced writer.

Despite the challenges of having thoughtful interactions with young writers, you'll no doubt also experience great joy as you sit alongside children who are making books. You'll be amazed at their insight, their courage, and their humor. You'll learn things about children—about their lives and their interests—that you might never have known if they didn't make books. And, of course, as Matt learned the day he ended up in a deep conversation about whether he was losing his hair or growing his hair, you never know where a conversation might wander along the way, so you learn to love the journey of talk you have with children too.

Meet Ben

Author and Illustrator of Spaceship

Ben is a child who loves engaging in many different activities in his preschool class, and he especially likes to build things and then play with his creations. Making books, however, is not an engagement he often chooses for himself.

One day Matt decided just to observe Ben for a while as he played in the classroom. After stopping in several different areas, Ben settled in with some Legos® and proceeded to build a spaceship. It had four Lego® passengers—a cat, a dog, Ben, and his dad. The passengers flew around the room on an imaginary mission.

Toward the end of the morning, Matt stopped Ben and asked him to tell him about what he'd been doing. Ben told Matt all about the spaceship, how he made it, and about the adventure the spaceship had inside a mountain. Matt told Ben he thought this was an interesting adventure story, and then he asked Ben some questions about the passengers. The two of them talked for some time about the spaceship.

Eventually, Matt asked Ben, "If you were going to make a book that would tell the story of the spaceship, what would you put on the first page?" Matt asked the question not so much because he wanted him to make this book, but just because he wanted Ben to consider the possibility. Ben, however, didn't respond to Matt's question. Instead, he went over to the writing area, got a blank book, sat down, and started an illustration on the first page.

Ben had the spaceship he'd made in front of him, and he carefully studied it as he added passengers to his illustration so that he could picture them in the correct order. If the reproduction of Ben's book were in color, you would see on the second page that the passengers (underneath the line for the spaceship) are each drawn to match the color they were in the Lego spaceship. With thoughtful, deliberate intention, Ben also drew them in the same colors on page four as they go into the mountain.

For Ben, this type of dramatic play proved a powerful support for his writing. Since he was the creator of the dramatic play, it was relatively easy for him to recreate this story in his book. And, because he is in a classroom environment that honors his approximations, Ben was able to engage in very complex decision making as he composed, long before he was able to make his illustrations and writing representational in any conventional sense.

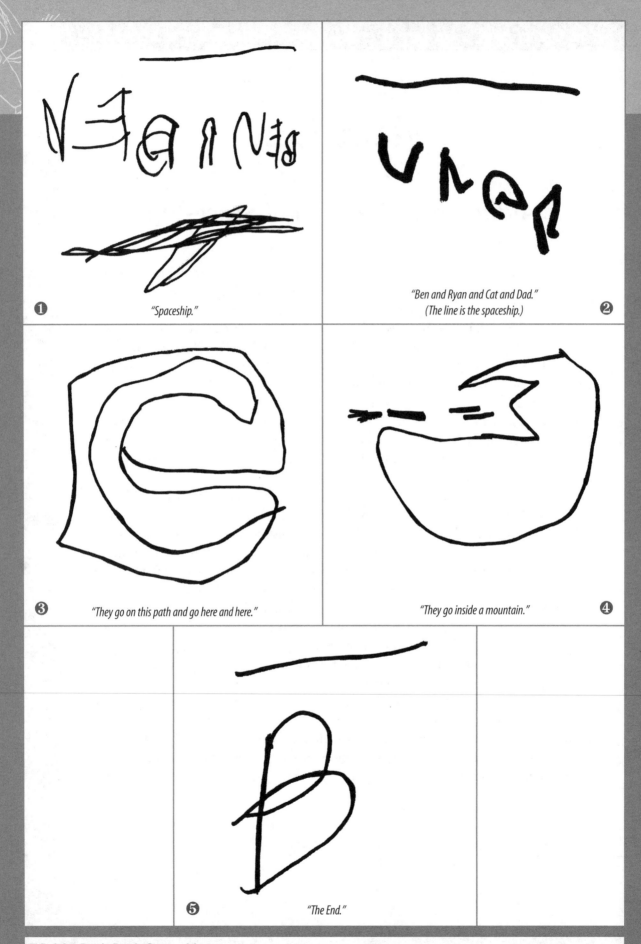

❶ *"Spaceship."*

❷ *"Ben and Ryan and Cat and Dad."*
(The line is the spaceship.)

❸ *"They go on this path and go here and here."*

❹ *"They go inside a mountain."*

❺ *"The End."*

FIG. 9.9 *Ben's Book,* Spaceship

Supporting Young Writers
with Share Time

At the end of a busy morning in early October, Matt sits with a whole class of preschoolers on their meeting carpet. Five of the children made books that morning, and Matt wants everyone to see those books. He starts by reminding them about the read-aloud book they shared earlier, and then he says, "Some of you were just like Mo Willems today. Mo Willems writes books, and you wrote books too." With this quick reminder, Matt supports the children in understanding their membership in the club of writers in the world. But the critical thing is that the books they are getting ready to see are written by writers who are actually a lot more like them than Mo Willems. The books they are going to see were written by other preschoolers sitting right next to them.

Kameron comes up first and stands beside Matt who is holding up his book about a giant so that everyone can see it (Figure 10.1). Because it is so early in the year, Matt provides lots of assistance as he and Kameron share the book. As they look at each page, Kameron says a little bit, and then Matt restates it in his best read-aloud voice, bringing the book to life for the other children. Over time, with lots of demonstrations of how to read and share books with others, Kameron and the other children will be able to do more and more of this sharing without the teacher's assistance, but for now, the sharing is very interactive.

When they've finished sharing the book, Matt points out two smart things Kameron did as a writer. He wrote his name on the cover, "just like Mo Willems puts his name on the cover," and, Matt says, "Isn't it smart how Kameron made his whole book be about just one thing. A giant. Every page is about the giant."

During the next few minutes, the other children's books are shared in much the same way, with Matt finding and pointing out something smart each child has done: Paige has an ending that comes back to her beginning idea; Nathan

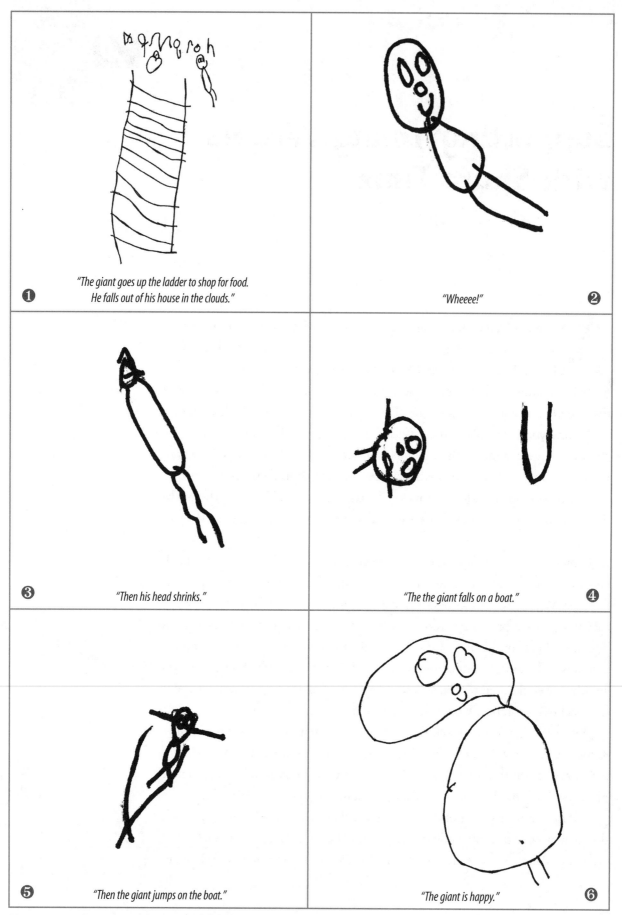

"The giant goes up the ladder to shop for food.
He falls out of his house in the clouds." ❶

"Wheeee!" ❷

"Then his head shrinks." ❸

"The the giant falls on a boat." ❹

"Then the giant jumps on the boat." ❺

"The giant is happy." ❻

FIG. 10.1 **Kameron's Book About a Giant**

uses two kinds of writing in his book—scribbles and print; Gracie's book, like Kameron's, stays with one idea; and Matthew's book about trees shows that he learned a book has to have more than one page (Figure 10.2). When he'd set out to write that day, Matthew had planned to draw an oak tree on a single page and let that be his whole book.

Over the course of a year, so much important teaching work happens around the simple routine of sharing preschoolers' books with other children. When teachers make time to celebrate smart thinking and initiative in this way, children come to understand that their work as writers is valued. We agree with Lillian Katz (1998) who says that children are incredibly savvy when it comes to knowing what the adults in their lives really value.

> However, the ability of young children to sense what the important adults in their lives really care about is likely to be universal. Thus all teachers might ask: What do most of my pupils really believe I take seriously and care deeply about? Awareness of what adults value should not be confused with what provokes adults' praise and flattery; rather, I have in mind children's awareness of what adults take seriously enough to make suggestions about, ask for clarification about, urge children to look again, reconsider, and perhaps do over again. (38)

Share time as a regular classroom routine teaches children so much about what teachers value in their work as writers, and this chapter considers the importance of share time as teaching time.

Understanding the Value of Share Time

The Purpose and Promise of Picture Books

When someone sets out to make a picture book, say a person like Denise Fleming or David Shannon, she or he imagines a future for that book that includes it being shared again and again with children. After all, that's what picture books are *for*—that's what they do in the world—just as other types of published writing are sent out with the hope that readers will find them. Denise and David wouldn't spend their time making picture books if they didn't expect anyone to read them.

For young writers like Kameron and Paige and Matthew to really understand what it is they are doing when they make picture books, over time they must come to expect that their books will be read. Leaving out that last

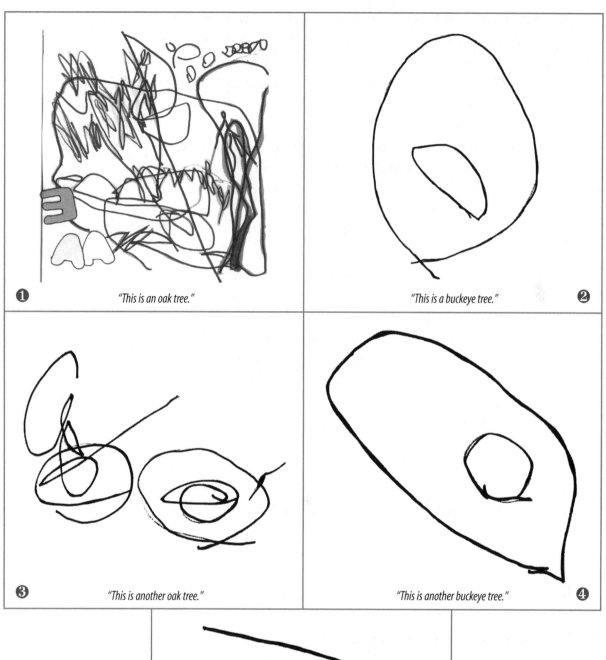

❶   *"This is an oak tree."*

❷   *"This is a buckeye tree."*

❸   *"This is another oak tree."*

❹   *"This is another buckeye tree."*

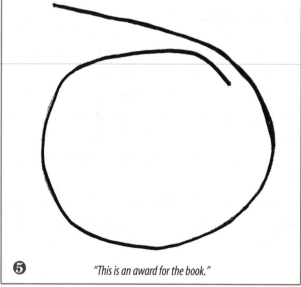

❺   *"This is an award for the book."*

FIG. 10.2   **Matthew's Book About Trees**

critical part of the process would be like baking cookies with children, taking the cookies out of the oven, and not eating them. Or preparing soil for a garden, planting seeds, and then forgetting to watch to see whether anything grows. The last steps are so critical to children understanding why they're doing the first steps.

The Christmas when Katie's nephew was two-and-a-half, he said basically the same thing every time he opened one of his presents. Eric would look at the unwrapped toy and say, "Dad, what it do?" For young children, understanding what things are for, understanding what they do, is such an important part of simply *understanding*. A picture book is for sharing, that's "what it do," and if a child makes one, he or she needs to see what it does to really understand what has been wrought.

The first reason, then, that finding some time to share children's books with other children is important is because it helps them understand the process of writing in a complete way. Sharing children's books helps them understand that writing ends with reading, and hopefully with readers laughing or sighing or exclaiming over something the writer has crafted, as the children laughed at Kameron's giant falling through the air and saying, "Wheeee!" Over time, as children experience the responses of others, they can begin to anticipate readers in much the same way experienced writers do.

Related to this, when the whole framework for helping children understand writing is built around connections to their reading—*Mo Willems makes books, and you can make books too*—then children need to see their books fulfilling the same purpose in the room as books made by professional authors and illustrators. Children need to see their books shared and enjoyed just like Mo Willems' books to understand their writing as being like the writing of this more experienced member of the club.

Our experience has been that most children like to come and stand by the teacher and help read and share from the books they've written, as Kameron did. Sometimes though, children express a desire for the teacher to read the book to the class while they remain seated. When children ask Matt to read their books without them, he almost always says, "Okay, but you let me know if I'm reading it right." He wants the children to know that he will read their books, but the words belong to them. Often, children do interrupt him and correct him, and many of them end up standing beside him before he's finished because they have trouble not engaging with the sharing of their own books in this way. As we said earlier, the goal is for children to carry more and more of the responsibility for reading their books during share time, though teachers will always be involved because they'll be highlighting the smart thinking children did as they composed.

Learning from Other Writers

One afternoon as Emma is sharing her book about bumble bees with the other children in her class, Jenna thinks out loud and says, to no one in particular, "Why can't I make a *B* like that?" From this comment, a short conversation ensues about how everyone is learning to write and they all make their writing a little differently. What is so telling about Jenna's comment is that she couldn't help but think about her own writing in light of Emma's. After all, Emma and Jenna have a lot in common as writers—they're both four, they're both in a class where they make books, and they've been part of the same conversations about writing. What Emma provided for Jenna on this day was a demonstration of what's possible in writing that was perfectly matched to Jenna's zone of proximal development. A room full of three- and four-year-old writers is ripe with demonstrations like this, and share time makes those demonstrations public and available.

As we explained in Chapter 7, everything children need to know about picture books can be found in them, and every time teachers share books with children, they are teaching them about this kind of text in the world. What children cannot learn from reading picture books, however, is what it's like to be *someone who is making a picture book* because the books that come from the store or the library are already finished. Children can't watch them being made. And, of course, the books that come from the store or the library were finished by very experienced writers.

How do children learn what it's like to be a preschooler and go through the process of making a picture book? They learn that from each other, and that is another important reason for sharing both their books and the smart thinking they engaged in while making them. This sharing helps children understand how other writers who are a lot like them go about making books.

Seeing picture books made by writers a lot like them also helps children have reasonable expectations for what their finished books should look like, and as we discussed in Chapter 8, this is a huge part of helping children believe they are capable writers. As books written and illustrated by different children are shared, over time they see a wide range of development represented in them, and they see their teachers confirming the smart thinking captured in each book. Seeing this, children come to understand their own writing and illustrating within the context of reasonable development, and most of them grow very comfortable with their abilities as writers within this context.

Once again, using the dimensions of composition development as a guide, teachers highlight preschoolers' smart decision making as they share their books with other children. This highlighting may range from noting that a three-year-old's book full of swirly lines in bright colors is "*all about* bright colors and beautiful swirly lines," a comment about focus, to noting a sophisticated revision strategy a child has used in moving a page in a book to a place where it makes more sense. The key for teachers is to learn to look at what a child's book shows she *does* know, and point this out, rather than focusing on what it shows she doesn't know. Sometimes, of course, this is more challenging than at other times, but as the dimensions of composition development become more and more operational in a teacher's thinking, it gets easier and easier to see what children's writing shows us they know.

Most of the time preschoolers finish making a book in one sitting, so most of the shared books are complete. Every now and then, though, a teacher will call children together for a share time and a child will have a book that's started but not finished. With the child's permission, teachers often go ahead and share these books because they help them demonstrate some of the thinking that happens in the middle of the process—most notably, thinking ahead about what one might write. Often, the teacher and the child share what has been done so far, and then with the other children, think about what the child might write tomorrow. Sometimes children don't go back to their books and finish them the next day, and sometimes they do, but the thinking demonstration does important teaching either way.

Here are some of the kinds of things teachers might call attention to in children's writing as it's shared. We won't include examples of each because most of them already can be seen in the many examples of children's writing throughout this book. A teacher might point out that in making a book, a child:

- Used both writing and illustrating

- Made the book all about one thing

- Organized the book either as a list or a story

- Used a lot of what the child knows about something to help come up with ideas

- Did something like a professional author does in a book the class has shared

- Learned something from another writer in the room

- Incorporated some feature of picture books, such as a title or author's name, on the front cover

- Did something on purpose to make the book more interesting

- Wrote in a specific genre

- Used a particular kind of writing, or more than one, in a book (highlighting the range of transcription development)

- Worked on a book for more than one day

- Has ideas for a book that's not finished

- Got an idea in a particular way or made a book for a specific reason

- Made a revision to clarify the ideas in a book

- Solved a problem encountered while writing

- Wrote a book that is similar or different from other books already written

Over time, as children's books are shared and their smart thinking is highlighted, a common language evolves around the process of writing. Children learn how to talk about writing in ways they probably don't have access to anywhere else. In the preschool classroom, using this language facilitates seamless movement from read-aloud, to side-by-side work with children, to share time. And talk, of course, is the vehicle for teaching, as we explained in Chapter 6, so what children learn to talk about, they simultaneously learn to *think* about.

Getting Ideas for Writing

As the class is sharing Alex's unfinished book about a monkey in a zoo and thinking about what else he might put on the blank pages, Evan spontaneously speaks up and says, "I want to make a book about a tiger." Apparently the energy he found in thinking about an animal in Alex's book made Evan think he'd like to make his own animal book.

In addition to learning about process from other preschoolers, another reason for sharing books is that children are often motivated to make books when they see what other children have made. This motivation probably stems from a combination of factors. Some children seem to be motivated by the idea of a book, as Evan was, and they want to make one about a similar idea. Certainly watching another child being the center of attention and receiving responses to a book makes some want that same experience for themselves; then too, some children are likely to be motivated by a belief that the process of making a book looks fun and engaging.

Connected to this, sometimes the sharing of books gets energy for making a particular kind of book going in the room. In one preschool class, the talk around two different how-to books one child made started a small landslide of ideas for other how-to books children might make: How to build a zoo with blocks, how to make a party, and how to work a camera were just a few of the ideas. Isabella's "how to do a snow dance" book, shown in Chapter 6, was written because of shared excitement around making this kind of book.

Usually when there is a buzz around a particular kind of book, talk about it is happening both at read-aloud time and at share time. This past year, a number of preschool classrooms experienced excitement about books that are made to teach people things. Teachers were sharing such books with children for a variety of curricular reasons, not just to support them as writers. Because the children had become so accustomed to making books like the ones their teachers read to them, they began making books that teach people things. Brooke's spider book (Figure 10.3) was made in a room where there was a lot of talk and energy about books that teach people things.

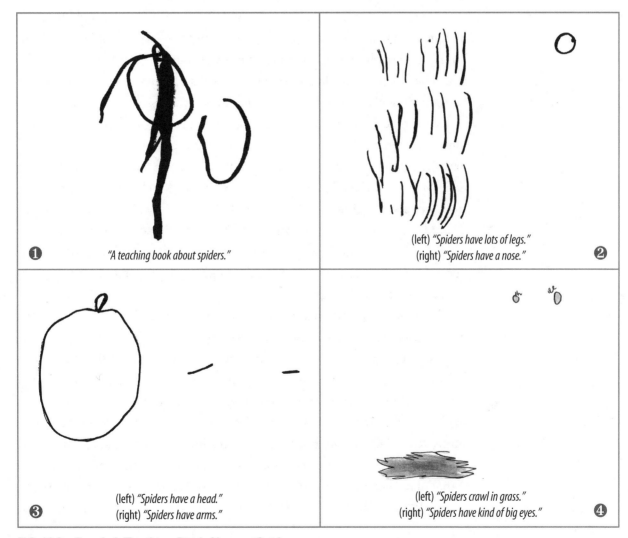

❶ *"A teaching book about spiders."*

(left) *"Spiders have lots of legs."*
(right) *"Spiders have a nose."* ❷

❸ (left) *"Spiders have a head."*
(right) *"Spiders have arms."*

(left) *"Spiders crawl in grass."*
(right) *"Spiders have kind of big eyes."* ❹

FIG. 10.3 *Brooke's Teaching Book About a Spider*

Sharing Supports Important Understandings About Reading

In Chapter 9, we discussed ways teachers can help children learn to read their books in side-by-side interactions, and we stressed the importance of repetition and rereading to help children hold their meanings constant over time. Usually, when a book is shared with the class, some time has passed since the child stopped working on it. That time may be as short as a few minutes or as long as a couple of days; either way, however, one of the critical understandings built as time passes is that the meaning stays constant and the book should be read the same way in subsequent readings.

Now, of course, teachers don't expect children to read books *exactly* the same way in a word-for-word sense. Without representative transcription and the ability to read it, keeping the words exact is difficult to do. Teachers simply want children to understand that the meaning in a book should be constant (even though the words may vary). In other words, if Kameron's book is about a giant shopping for food and falling from the sky when he writes it, it should be about a giant shopping for food and falling from the sky when he reads it. Understanding this about their own writing, of course, is very connected to the emergent storybook reading so many children do as they read familiar picture books again and again and learn to keep the story the same with each reading.

Early in the year, children may need lots of support to read their books in the same way they read them as they were writing them, but with assistance and experience, they will grow to understand constancy of meaning over time. In early May when Katie observed in different preschool classrooms during share time, not a single child in more than a dozen altered the basic meaning of his or her book as it was shared; this was true across a broad developmental spectrum. By this point in the year, children at very different places in their development all demonstrated a clear understanding of the essential relationship between writing and reading.

Share time, and particularly the distance it creates between the act of writing and the act of reading, helps children build a solid understanding of the constancy of meaning, and it also helps children learn to read their texts with meaning. Teachers should be careful to demonstrate reading in a meaningful, read-aloud voice when they assist children in sharing their books. Kameron, for instance, said *"Wheeee!"* in a very flat, unanimated voice when Matt first turned to that page in his book. His reading certainly didn't match his intended meaning—that a giant was falling from the sky! Matt asked Kameron if that's how he thought the giant would sound if he was falling, and he shook his head "No." Matt then reread the page and filled the word with the intended meaning, stretching it out so it truly sounded as if it was said by someone who was falling.

When sharing preschoolers' books, many opportunities exist to demonstrate reading with meaning for children. Sometimes the demonstration is of very simple text, but the teacher crafts her reading with pitch and intonation so that it sounds like something one might read in a book: *I am smelling a pretty flower.* However the page should be read, the first key is to help children hear and understand what reading sounds like, and that it's different from just talking.

The second key, of course, is to help children learn to read in a way that conveys their intended meanings. If what is happening in the story line is exciting, then the sound of the reading should convey that. If the meaning is sad, the reading should convey that. If the book is a teaching book, then the facts should be read clearly and distinctly, like facts. If children come to understand as writers that reading means not just saying the words, but saying them the way you mean them, this certainly will also nudge their development along as readers in significant ways.

A Context for Ongoing Composition and Revision

When teachers work side by side with those who are making books, they often see that as they talk with children and engage them in repeated readings of their books, the texts become more elaborate with each reading. It's not that the meaning changes; it's that it develops more with each reading, the talk serving as a form of rehearsal. The same thing often happens when children read their books during share time. While the basic meaning is intact, the child's reading is embellished and actually sounds more like a book. Reading in front of an audience probably encourages some children to revise and compose new text as they share their books, and many no doubt learn a lot from watching the demonstrations of other children reading their books.

Reading in front of an audience also seems to help some children pull their ideas together into a more coherent text. As Matt sat beside Catherine one afternoon, she worked on a book about jewelry. The first language Catherine used to read her book was labeling language: "I wear bracelets on my hands. I wear earrings on my ears." But as she continued to work on the book, it became clear that she was moving toward a more narrative composition. Her mom was pictured on one page, and a store was pictured on another. In her conversation with Matt, though, the narrative as a whole was never really made clear. Perhaps there was so much talk around it that Catherine struggled to make the ideas connect.

Interestingly, when share time came, Catherine confidently shared her book and connected all the ideas into a coherent reading (Figure 10.4). She even used words like *so* and *now* to indicate the key time relationships in the narrative. The on-the-spot, uninterrupted sort of reading that children understand is expected during share time seems to help some of them pull their ideas together in a more finished way.

Whether it's adding details to make a book more interesting or pulling all the pieces together to make a book sound more like a book, teachers embrace and support the continued composition and revision that many children do as they share their books. The routine of sharing books is valuable in part because it creates another context where children's composition development is so clearly supported.

❶ *"The girl needed some new jewelry."*

❷ *"So she went out the door with her mom."*

❸ *"And she went out to the store."*

❹ *"Now she has new orange jewelry."*

FIG. 10.4 **Catherine's Book About Shopping for Jewelry**

Building Identities and Histories as Writers

On the same morning as the share time recounted at the beginning of this chapter, as the children were leaving from read-aloud to go out and play in the room, Matt told them that if any of them decided to make books while they were playing, he wanted to watch. The children's teacher spoke up and told Matt he would love watching them make books because they make great books. She said, "I remember a book Nathan wrote about spaghetti and another one about pizza. I remember that. That book made me hungry. And do you remember Kameron's monster book? Wasn't it scary?"

The teacher's comments about books children have made in the past are significant on several levels. First, comments like these help children understand the permanent nature of book-making. A book that has been written and shared *exists* in a permanent way, not only the book itself but also the memory of it in readers' minds: *"That book made me hungry."* So many of children's activities are temporal in nature—a child builds something with blocks and it's torn down before anyone sees it; an elaborate scene is created in dramatic play, and the next day a totally new scene evolves. But when children make books and those books are shared with others, the experience of "having written" lives on. Creating a public, shared memory of a book that's been written is important because it helps children understand one of the most basic functions of written language: to create a record that holds fast throughout time.

The teacher's comments hint at another very important reason for sharing children's books. When books are made public, children's identities as writers are nurtured. Nathan is a writer who makes people hungry with his books. Emma is a writer who makes really good B's. Brooke knows a lot about spiders and teaches people about them in her books. Catherine is a fashion writer with her books about jewelry. Matthew writes award-winning books about trees. Kameron is a writer of scary books about monsters. Perhaps Kameron's decision later that morning to make a book about a giant falling from the sky was in part motivated by this identity his teacher named for him. Writers, both those with lots of experience and those who are just starting out, come to be known by what they publish.

Once children's books have been shared and everyone knows about them, teachers continue to refer to them, making connections to other books and conversations about books, both professional picture books and those made by children. As the leaves begin to turn in the fall, for example, a teacher might share from Doris Gove's picture book *My Mother Talks to Trees* (1999) and remind the children that Matthew wrote a book about trees too, oak trees and buckeye trees. Keeping past books in the collective consciousness of the classroom helps maintain children's identities as authors of books and also supports their understandings about the permanency of authorship over time.

All Writers Should Be So Lucky

As one of Katie's favorite writers, Pulitzer Prize–winning journalist Leonard Pitts says (2004), "Idealistic young scribes who insist their work is for them alone will disagree, but a writer without readers is like a person shouting in an empty room." We end, then, with the simplest, most logical reason to find time to share children's books: We don't want young writers left to shout into empty rooms. Writers need readers, and they need them whether they are Pulitzer Prize winners or three-year-olds who draw their own medals on their books.

Meet Parker

Author and Illustrator of Penguins

Since early in the year, Parker and his classmates showed an interest in animals. The children created elaborate zoos in the block area. They drew animals from observation and sculpted animals out of clay. Naturally, they created lots of stories about animals during their dramatic play and in the books they made.

Later in the year, Parker's class began reading more nonfiction books and doing more research from books on animals and zoos. The children became very familiar with the features of nonfiction books, and several wrote their own to share their extensive animal knowledge.

One day, the class had read a new nonfiction book full of interesting facts about animals. At the end of the read-aloud, the teacher talked a little about the difference between nonfiction books that teach you something and narrative books that tell you a story. She reminded the children that if they wrote a book that day, they would need to think about which type of book they wanted to write. After a brief discussion about some topics for books they might write, the children went off into the room to begin their morning of play and exploration.

Several children went straight to the writing center and started working on books on a variety of topics, including several featured in earlier chapters of this book: Charlie's *Colors* book (Figure 5.2), Julia's *Zoo Animals* book (Figure 6.3), and Pravnov's *Solar System* book (Figure 9.5). After spending some time in different areas of the room, Parker came over and joined the group at the writing table. As he sat down he announced he was going to make a book about penguins. When asked what kind of a book, he said it was going to be a book that teaches people about penguins. Parker talked about the many penguin facts he knew and how they might go into his book.

The opening pages sound like a nonfiction book, with facts about how penguins slide on their bellies and eat fish, but in the midst of his composing, Parker's narrative instincts took over—no doubt supported by the rich storytelling experiences he'd had throughout the year. His book shifts into full story mode as his penguins encounter a bear, run for their lives, and dance with glee when they're safe. Parker uses crafting techniques he's seen in other books, including speech bubbles with dialogue between characters.

Parker set out with one intention and ended up following another—an experience many writers have at one time or another. After all, sometimes the writing just leads the writer in a different direction than was expected. Parker's readers were certainly grateful he let his writing lead him—the story part of *Penguins* was quite a hit with both adults and children in his class.

FIG. 10.5 *Parker's Book,* **Penguins**

Afterword

■■■■■■■■■■■■■■■■■■■■■■■■■■■■■■■■

Throughout *Already Ready*, we've talked many times about the fine art of all this teaching, about knowing the difference between nudging and pushing, and about knowing when to let go and being willing to do it. As we come to this closing section, we realize, perhaps, that this is the fine art of writing too.

In light of this realization, we come to a close with things left unsaid and questions yet to be considered, but perhaps enough is enough. Our hope is that what we *have* said and what we *have* discussed in this book will, in a small way, nudge professional conversations forward as they relate to the literate lives of children. Our hope is that other teachers will continue to add their experiences and insights to the conversations.

We know there are many avenues yet to explore. For example, in our future work, we'd like to think more about the following:

- ❧ The language of side-by-side teaching: The margins of the many pages of transcripts we have of this teaching are simply filled with questions and comments about what teachers say and why they say certain things in particular ways.

- ❧ The role of classroom exploration, particularly dramatic play, as a motivating spark for young writers: "Living" a topic seems to provide an important sort of rehearsal for writing about a topic, at least for many children.

- ❧ The relationship between composition development and oral language development—particularly as children search for words to capture the meanings in their illustrations and connect them across pages.

- The children with special needs and how they might be better supported as writers.

- The impact of preschool writing experiences on later development: While we value these experiences for how they enrich children's lives right now, we cannot help but wonder what these children will be like as writers in two or three or four more years.

Questions like these will no doubt keep us involved in the serious study of children (Malaguzzi 1998) for a long, long time.

Nothing Less Than Perfect

And finally, one last story. One last thought . . .

Matt is talking with a group of preschoolers about Nicola Smee and her book *Clip-Clop!* while he is reading them the author's note where it says Nicola began writing books when she was four years old. One child says, almost immediately, "Hey, I'm four." And then suddenly there is a chorus ringing out: "I'm three!" "I'm four!" "I'm four-and-a-half." In the midst of this chorus, Kara gestures with both her hands out in front of her and says, "This is perfect!"

After watching and studying hours and hours of videotaped classroom interactions, for us, this single moment stands out above all others. We could watch it over and over and it would never fail to awaken in us a sense of larger purpose about the important, life-altering work teachers do with the young children in their care. We love the spirit of this moment—the sudden realization of how perfect it all is, that the author of a book the children love so much that they know the words by heart started writing when she was four years old. *Just like us. It's perfect.*

We leave this moment with you in the hope that the spirit of it is the spirit you take away from this book. We hope our desire to help children find *perfect* places to live and grow as writers has been clear from start to . . . finish.

Lakota Early Childhood Center News

Lakota Early Childhood Center NEWS

Dear Parents,

"Are you a writer?" What an important question for a 5 year old to ask.

A couple of weeks ago Bethany, a kindergarten student, was sitting next to a 2nd grade teacher at a football game. Bethany had taken some paper with her to the game and she was drawing and writing. A man sitting behind Bethany saw what she was doing and he drew a picture for her.

Bethany leaned into him and asked, "Are you a writer?"

"No," the man replied.

Bethany then asked the 2nd grade teacher the same question, and the teacher enthusiastically replied, "Yes!"

Bethany said, "Good, then I can tell you my secret. All books have pictures *and* words."

The two "writers" engaged in more insider talk about the world of writing. They were both part of the same club, the club of people who see themselves as writers, people who know things about how writing works.

The teacher then told Bethany that the man was a writer too. He just didn't know he was a writer; he writes letters and lists and plans. Bethany was excited to be able to share her important knowledge with him as well.

This interaction between these two writers is significant because of what it tells us about Bethany's image of herself as a writer. She thinks of herself as someone who writes, someone who makes books. She sees herself as someone who knows the tricks of the trade about writing just like a professional writer would. And she knows that she can act like a writer and share this important knowledge with others.

In order for children to see themselves as writers, adults must also see them as writers. This sometimes takes a leap of faith as adults look at their writing approximations, their scribbles and their beginning attempts at spelling. But isn't that where we all start when we try something new? Whether it's golfing or knitting or dancing, when we first try something new we approximate doing it. If we're encouraged, we're likely to continue to try and learn. If not, our initial enthusiasm can be quickly dashed. In fact, our early approximations show what we know, as well as what we need to learn next. But first we need to see ourselves as golfers or knitters or dancers, just like children who are learning to see themselves as writers.

Recently, Olivia, a 3 year old preschooler, was reading a book she had written at school, *Scary Bear, Nice Bear*, to her family at home. She read it just like a writer would, using inflection, holding the book so her family could see her illustrations, pointing out details on each page. Olivia wants to take her creation to her grandparents and read it to them. Olivia certainly sees herself as a writer. Olivia's mother stated it best when she said, "Already an author at age 3."

How fortunate for Olivia and Bethany that the importance of this self image is recognized, celebrated, and nurtured.

Sincerely,

Matt Glover

Important!!
Kindergarten Drop Off

Recently Kindergarten parents have been dropping off earlier and earlier. This causes a serious problem for preschool students who are arriving late to school even though they were in line on time.

Kindergarten parents, in order to ensure that preschool children are on time, please, do not get in the car line until:

AM Session 9:15
PM Session 1:10

Preschool parents should always have their preschool sign on their dashboard.

Composition Dimensions

Teachers: Here are the composition dimension questions all on one page. You can copy it and use as a reminder when you're considering possible "composition nudges" for young writers.

Understandings About Texts

- *Is the child's book about something?*
- *How has the child organized the book? Does it move through time (narrative) or through a list of ideas (nonnarrative)?*
- *When the child reads it does it sound like a book?*
- *Does the child read the book basically the same way over time?*
- *Is the child making the book in the manner of other picture books he or she has seen?*
- *What does the book show the child understands about genre?*
- *How is the child representing meaning in the book?*

Understandings About Process

- *Is the child intentional about what is being represented on the page?*
- *Does the child engage in revision while composing a picture book?*
- *Is there any evidence that the child is thinking ahead about what to write next?*
- *Has the child made any intentional crafting decisions in the book?*
- *How long has the child worked on the book? In one sitting? Over time?*
- *Does the child show a willingness to solve problems while writing?*

Understandings About What It Means to Be a Writer

- *How (and why) has the child decided what to write about in the book?*
- *How interested is the child in an audience's response to the book?*
- *Has the child composed in a way that leads to new meaning while writing?*
- *Can I see in the book that the child has been willing to take compositional risks?*
- *As I interact with the child around the book, does it seem that he or she has a sense of self as a writer? A sense of history?*
- *Does the child show she understands her powerful position as author of the book?*

Works Cited

■■■■■■■■■■■■■■■■■■■■■■■■■■■■■■■■■■■■

Professional Literature

Barnes, D. 1992. *From Communication to Curriculum*, Second Edition. Portsmouth, NH: Heinemann.

Bissex, G. 1980. *GNYS at Work: A Child Learns to Write and Read*. Cambridge, MA: Harvard University Press.

Bomer, R. 2006. Session at Conference of the National Council of Teachers of English. Nashville, TN.

Calkins, L. 1994. *The Art of Teaching Writing*, Second Edition. Portsmouth, NH: Heinemann.

Clay, M. 1975. *What Did I Write?* Auckland, New Zealand: Heinemann.

Costa, A. L., and B. Kallick, eds. 2000. *Discovering and Exploring Habits of Mind*. Alexandria, VA: ASCD.

Dorn, L., and C. Soffos. 2001. *Scaffolding Young Writers: A Writers' Workshop Approach*. Portland, ME: Stenhouse.

Dyson, A. H. 1993. *Social Worlds of Children Learning to Write*. New York: Teachers College Press.

Edwards, C., L. Gandini, and G. Forman, eds. 1998. *The Hundred Languages of Children: The Reggio Emilia Approach—Advanced Reflections*, Second Edition. Westport, CT: Ablex Publishing.

Ferreiro, E., and A. Teberosky. 1982. *Literacy Before Schooling*. Portsmouth, NH: Heinemann.

Gardner, H. 1998. "Foreword: Complementary Perspectives on Reggio Emilia." In *The Hundred Languages of Children: The Reggio Emilia Approach—*

Advanced Reflections, Second Edition, edited by C. Edwards, L. Gandini, and G. Forman, xv–xviii. Westport, CT: Ablex Publishing.

Gentry, R., and J. W. Gillet. 1993. *Teaching Kids to Spell*. Portsmouth, NH: Heinemann.

Halliday, M. 1975. *Learning How to Mean: Explorations in the Development of Language*. London: Edward Arnold.

Harste, J., V. Woodward, and C. Burke. 1984. *Language Stories and Literacy Lessons*. Portsmouth, NH: Heinemann.

Helm, J. H., and L. Katz. 2001. *Young Investigators: The Project Approach in the Early Years*. New York: Teachers College Press.

Henderson, E., and J. Beers, eds. 1980. *Developmental and Cognitive Aspects of Learning to Spell*. Newark, DE: International Reading Association.

Johnston, P. 2004. *Choice Words: How Our Language Affects Children's Learning*. Portland, ME: Stenhouse.

Katz, L. 1998. "What Can We Learn from Reggio Emilia?" In *The Hundred Languages of Children: The Reggio Emilia Approach—Advanced Reflections*, Second Edition, edited by C. Edwards, L. Gandini, and G. Forman, 27–45. Westport, CT: Ablex Publishing.

Malaguzzi, L. 1998. "History, Ideas and Basic Philosophy: An Interview with Lella Gandini." In *The Hundred Languages of Children: The Reggio Emilia Approach—Advanced Reflections*, Second Edition, edited by C. Edwards, L. Gandini, and G. Forman, 49–97. Westport, CT: Ablex Publishing.

NAEYC. 1997. *Developmentally Appropriate Practice in Early Childhood Programs Serving Children from Birth Through Age 8: A Position Statement of the National Association for the Education of Young Children*. Washington, DC: NAEYC.

NAEYC and IRA. 2005. *Where We Stand on Learning to Read and Write: A Joint Position Statement of the National Association for the Education of Young Children and the International Reading Association*. Online: www.naeyc.org/about/positions/asp.

Pitts, L. 2004 (April 9). "My First Reader." *The Miami Herald*.

Ray, K. W. 1999. *Wondrous Words: Writers and Writing in the Elementary Classroom*. Urbana, IL: National Council of Teachers of English.

———. 2001. *The Writing Workshop: Working Through the Hard Parts (and They're All Hard Parts)*. With writers voices by L. Laminack. Urbana, IL: National Council of Teachers of English.

———. 2006. *Study Driven: A Framework for Planning Units of Study in the Writing Workshop*. Portsmouth, NH: Heinemann.

Ray, K. W., with L. Cleaveland. 2004. *About the Authors: Writing Workshop with Our Youngest Writers*. Portsmouth, NH: Heinemann.

Read, C. 1971. "Pre-school Children's Knowledge of English Phonology." *Harvard Educational Review* 41: 1–34.

Rowe, D. W. 1994. *Preschoolers as Authors: Literacy Learning in the Social World of the Classroom*. Cresskill, NJ: Hampton Press.

Schickendanz, J. 1999. *Much More Than the ABCs*. Washington, DC: National Association for the Education of Young Children.

Smith, F. 1988. *Joining the Literacy Club*. Portsmouth, NH: Heinemann.

Sulzby, E. 1989. "Assessment of Writing and of Children's Language While Writing." In *The Role of Assessment and Measurement in Early Literacy Instruction*, edited by L. M. Morrow and J. Smith, 83–109. Englewood Cliffs, NJ: Prentice-Hall.

Sulzby, E., and W. Teale. 1985. "Writing Development in Early Childhood." *Educational Horizons* 64: 8–12.

Vygotsky, L. 1978. *Mind in Society: The Development of Higher Psychological Processes*, edited by M. Cole, V. John-Steiner, S. Scribner, and E. Souberman. Cambridge, MA: Harvard University Press.

———. 1986. *Thought and Language*, revised edition, edited by A. Kozulin. Cambridge, MA: The MIT Press.

Wilde, S. 1992. *You Kan Red This!* Portsmouth, NH: Heinemann.

Trade Books

Adams, D. 2005. *Zoom!* Illus. by Kevin Luthardt. Atlanta: Peachtree.

Aston, D. 2006. *An Egg Is Quiet*. Illus. by Sylvia Long. San Francisco: Chronicle Books.

Barton, B. 1982. *Airport*. New York: HarperTrophy.

Bauer, M. D. 1997. *If You Were Born a Kitten*. Illus. by JoEllen M. Stammen. New York: Simon & Shuster.

Beaumont, K. 2002. *Being Friends*. Illus. by Joy Allen. New York: Dial.

Bloom, S. 2005. *A Splendid Friend, Indeed*. Honesdale, PA: Boyds Mills Press.

Broach, E. 2005. *Wet Dog!* Illus. by David Catrow. New York: Dial.

Carle, E. 2000. *Dream Snow*. New York: Philomel.

Carlson, N. 1988. *I Like Me!* New York: Puffin.

Cooper, E. 2006. *Beach*. New York: Orchard Books.

Cowley, J. 2005. *Chameleon, Chameleon*. Photos by Nic Bishop. New York: Scholastic Press.

Crews, D. 1978. *Freight Train*. New York: Greenwillow.

———. 1998. *Night at the Fair*. New York: Greenwillow.

———. 1983. *Parade*. New York: Greenwillow.

———. 1995. *Sail Away*. New York: Greenwillow.

Fisher, V. 2002. *My Big Brother*. New York: Atheneum.

Frazee, M. 2003. *Roller Coaster*. New York: Harcourt

———. 2006. *Walk On! A Guide for Babies of All Ages*. New York: Harcourt.

Gore, S. 1995. *My Cake*. Illustrated by Fiona Pragoff. Strongsville, OH: Gareth Stevens Publishing.

Gove, D. 1999. *My Mother Talks to Trees*. Illus. by Marilynn Mallory. Atlanta: Peachtree.

Graham, B. 2001. *"Let's Get a Pup!" Said Kate*. Cambridge, MA: Candlewick Press.

Hubbell, P. 2003. *Trucks: Whizz! Zoom! Rumble!* Illus. by Megan Halsey. New York: Marshall Cavendish Corporation.

Isadora, R. 1999. *Sophie Skates*. New York: Puffin.

Jenkins, S. 1995. *Biggest, Fastest, Strongest*. New York: Houghton Mifflin.

Karas, G. B. 2005. *On Earth*. New York: G. P. Putnam's Sons.

Keats, E. J. 1967. *Peter's Chair*. New York: HarperCollins.

Krull, K. 2001. *Supermarket*. Illus. by Melanie Hope Greenburg. New York: Holiday House.

Levenson, G. 1999. *Pumpkin Circle*. Berkeley, CA: Tricycle Press.

———. 2004. *Bread Comes to Life*. Photos by Shmuel Thaler. Berkeley, CA: Tricycle Press.

Long, M. 2003. *How I Became a Pirate*. Illus. by David Shannon. New York: Harcourt Children's Books.

Mayo, M. 2002. *Dig, Dig, Digging*. Illus. by Alex Ayliffe. New York: Henry Holt & Co.

McMullan, K. and J. 2002. *I Stink!* New York: Joanna Cotler Books.

Murphy, M. 1997. *I Like It When . . .* New York: Harcourt, Brace & Company.

Partridge, E. 2003. *Whistling*. Illus. by Anna G. Hines. New York: Greenwillow.

Pham, L. 2005. *Big Sister, Little Sister*. New York: Hyperion.

Reynolds, P. H. 2004. *Ish*. Cambridge, MA: Candlewick Press.

Root, P. 2001. *Rattletrap Car*. Illus. by Jill Barton. Cambridge, MA: Candlewick Press.

Schaefer, A. R. 2004. *Roller Coaster Wild Rides*. Mankato, MN: Capstone Press.

Shannon, D. 1998. *No, David!* New York: Blue Sky Press.

———. 2002. *Duck on a Bike*. New York: Blue Sky Press.

Smee, N. 2006. *Clip-Clop!* London: Boxer Books.

Sweeney, J. 1999. *Me and My Amazing Body*. Illus. by Annette Cable. New York: Knopf Books for Young Readers.

Waddell, M. 1992. *Owl Babies*. Illus. by P. Benson. Cambridge, MA: Candlewick Press.

Wilde, M. 1994. *Our Granny*. Illus. by Julie Vivas. Boston: Houghton Mifflin.

Willems, M. 2003. *Don't Let the Pigeon Drive the Bus*. New York: Hyperion.

———. 2004. *Knuffle Bunny*. New York: Hyperion.

———. 2005. *Leonardo the Terrible Monster*. New York: Hyperion.

Wood, A. 1992. *Silly Sally*. New York: Harcourt, Brace, Jovanovich.

Index